Ashes In My Skull

Ashes In My Skull

poems by

Thomas Walker

Thomas Walker Publications

Eagle River, Alaska

Ashes In My Skull

Library of Congress Control Number: 2012906937
ISBN 978-0615628615

Thomas Walker Publications
Eagle River, Alaska
www.thomas-walker-institute.com

Email: contact@thomas-walker-institute.com

To
anyone who cares.

I am the Neptune King,
cast forever a luster of shadowy blue
in the soft-lit eyes of the universe,
desperately seeking to erase 'the curse'
of riding in the back of Erato's hearse.
Life could not get too much worse,
or so I verse......
or so I verse…...

Contents

Ashes In My Skull

You are the Evening Star

I thought my world
had finally come to end.
I searched, I searched,
but could find no friend.

You took me in,
a bird with a broken wing,
knowing I needed
more than a one night fling.

You warded off
the phantom of persuasions,
who convinced me
to give up life's sensations.

You are the one
with a touch that can repair,
my dying heart,
by showing how much you care.

It is only a theory,
but I do think,
the universe began
with a gentle blink,

when Venus took Neptune
for a midnight swim,
and said for the first time
that she loved him.

Five Minutes With You

Golden immaculate beauty,
let me bend......the rules;
let me spend......even just five minutes with you.

1---Even just five minutes with you,
        makes night turn to day,
        takes the rain clouds away,
        and in a field of daisies I lay.

2---Even just five minutes with you,
        and I am in too deep,
        mine is yours to keep,
        I am falling into sleep.

3---Even just five minutes with you,
        makes me slip into a dream,
        under a tree down by a stream,
        where your sunshine does gleam.

4---Even just five minutes with you,
        lifts my feet up off the floor,
        and like the eagle I soar,
        to a far and distant shore.

5---Even just five minutes with you,
        makes something happen inside,
        you take me for a ride,
        and across the stars I glide.

Golden immaculate beauty,
let me bend......the rules;
let me spend......even just five minutes with you.

Curls of Gold

Desperation, a plasma sensation,
a notched out skull of embedded hate
with sleepy hollow ice trays
pouring out nocturnal enemies,
listening, in spite of the spine tingling,
slithering Grass Dweller
puncturing Lilliputian dreams.
While harbor boats capsize
on a calm winter day,
hypnotic Hippocrates hymns
are sung out of key.
Arctic oxen, uniformly
overtaken by a powerful mistress,
a copulating fantasia seed.
But feeling good is all we knead,
like dough, until it is smooth.
The united sharing palpable scenes
tucked away neatly with
every day's same old magic beans.
Now I don't blame Jack for wanting gold,
or Goldie for fondling porridge cold;
desiring plantlike plasticine formations,
burning forever in memory citations.
Flowing slowly, flowing free,
and bonding by the hour
in frontal view of me,
a caged beauty
full of milky virtuosity.
Let us merge and give rise
to the unstoppable spurge.

......and?

Meanwhile......

I tried and tried to let her know
that all in all, we can't let go;
some things are bound together by wine.
A little out of touch, so it seems;
infinity walks on the beams
connected from your heart to mine.

It is the same old thing every day;
no clouds above, but the sky is grey
when I wake up without you by my side.
I don't believe in poetry and gods and fate
and time and hope and lies and hate;
but by the labours of love, I will abide.

I believe in flowers;
I believe in roses;
I believe in butterflies
and naked eyes and naked eyes and naked eyes;
in the sun,
in the moon,
......and making love
on a rainy afternoon.

I believe in colors;
I believe in rainbows;
I believe in red birds
and white birds and blue birds and black birds;
in the sky,
in the trees,
......and walking on the beach
with a cool autumn breeze.

I believe in beauty;
I believe in romance;
I believe in emotion
and passion and passion and passion;
in the touch,
in the kiss,
.....and divine memories
that we'll reminisce.

I believe in smiles;
I believe in magic;
I believe in destiny
and unity and unity and unity;
in the thought,
in the dream,
......and floating down
an endless one-way stream.

I believe in freedom,
I believe in love,
I believe in free-love
and free-love and free-love and free-love;
the love in you,
the love in me,
......and that
is just reality.

The Sky is A-falling

Oh Vanessa, oh Vanessa,
I know you'd like to be free;
to get whatever you want,
be whatever you want to be;
but I have to confess,
you are the only one for me;
for my heart never lies......
down at the bottom of the sea.

I'm so very tired,
woke up this morning at sunrise;
tossing and turning all night,
barely even shut my eyes;
isn't it funny how the mind races,
and the time, it flies;
when you're in love and free,
when you're in love like me.

Oh Vanessa, oh Vanessa,
my heart cannot be wrong;
the candles are burning
and my desire is strong;
to taste you, to touch you,
to sing you my song;
girl you're on my mind;
all of the night and all day long.

I can't stop thinking of you,
I just need a chance;
to show you my soul,
to show you romance;
isn't it funny how the eyes sing,
while the heart does dance;
when you're in love and free,
when you're in love like me.

Oh Vanessa, oh Vanessa,
the window is open wide;
and the wind won't stop howling,
until you'll be my bride;
a hand full of emotion,
all locked up inside;
your body is a vision of love,
so soft, so sweet, with nothing to hide.

I'm so very tired,
I lay myself down to rest;
knowing I will only get,
a few hours of sleep at best;
isn't it funny how you feel,
that pounding in your chest;
when you're in love and free,
when you're in love like me.

Oh Vanessa, oh Vanessa,
if you only knew;
all of the inhibitions
that I have for you;
then Vanessa, oh Vanessa,
you'd know that it is true;
the sky is a-falling
and I'm falling too;
a-falling......
a-falling......
in love with you!

Stones of Innocence

Be the receiver of my triumph
oh, oiled Empress.
Let us rejoice in the symmetry
of the sunflower circles.
Your divinity corners me.
Your divinity leads me
walking blindly on passion's ledge
as I watch your hand,
up and down sanctuary's flesh,
like a razor's edge.

Your eyes of onyx,
so deep, reflecting thoughts of intimacy;
such a potent sedation.
Your spiritual uniqueness,
so delicate like glass;
the stones of innocence
waiting to leave you shattered.
You knew all along what was coming,
but it never really mattered;
you longed to be left with the shards.
Passing on the laurel crown,
you've stolen the key from the guards,
the guards of erotic glories.
Sipping from the chalice of the gods,
you reveal secret stories;
your daffodil lips transfer vibrant energy.
Be the receiver of my triumph
oh, oiled Empress.

The Saint

The silence opens a door;
two dozen roses carefully laid out on the floor,
pink and luminous, forming the words: LOVE IS.
A heart appears like a momentary eclipse
then sunshine/romance; virtuosity tempting misery,
feed her with your own hands.
(but seriously)
Why couldn't we hear the change?
Why hasn't anyone else?
(the madness is infectious......)
Let me sleep and once again be stable
in my hopeless individual isolation.

Another love gone by, another well gone dry,
another planet gone awry.
Look into the eye......of my pipe,
burn-n-breathe the story of the Saint
who dreamed away the day he died
and lived his life on infinity's side.
Don't ever let anyone tell you
that it is impossible to dream,
because forever is just a black rose......
a memory lodged between each and every day
that somebody makes you want to give up.

Oh, desert rose, come and take me home,
away from here so I can roam.
It is said that a dog whose been beaten down
will learn to live before he leaves town.
Hey, hey lady, isn't it plain to see
that you are the reason for my misery.
Yet, a poet and a broken pen
are the reasons I will come and come back again.

All I Have to Offer is My Love

Reach.
Reach.
Reach.
Reach for me.
Reach for me,
way down below.
I want to fill your hollow soul,
cut my finger,
see my blood
dripping on the white winter dove.

Fly.
Fly.
Fly.
Fly red dove, fly.
Fly far away
to yesteryear and say......goodbye my love.
Isn't it funny how
when things don't go our way we cry,
and
when things don't go your way, you die.

Desert......save me.
Desert......kill me,
blazing burrows beneath these sands,
the willow moans,
'I think I can......
come into your hollow soul......'

Dionysian expedites.
Dionysian expedites
travel with me through ancient vision,
passion and pearls, a final decision.
Sunflowers circle the white knight's sword,
ecstasy reaching a divinely lord.

Ashes In My Skull

It is all around, it is all around,
but it is not easily found
unless you have platinum in your pockets,
and your nose to the ground.

All a woman has to do is just ask,
and a man will put on his mask......of love.
A man has to do more than just ask,
he has to make an offer.

Every woman has her price.
You'll have to pay......for sacrifice.
Every woman can make it to the show,
if she can perform the song of overflow.

Gallows of Despair: the song of Escapade

Life has its hands wrapped around my throat,
clenched so tight I think I'm gonna......
CHOKE;
I hope it's just a joke, just a joke.
I'm so lonely, I'm so damned tired,
I feel like I'm a sacrificial......
LAMB;
is that all that I am, all that I am.

I am at the final crossroad but,
I can't decide which way to......
TURN;
without feeling the burn, feeling the burn.
I don't want anything at all yet,
I know what I need, I need to......
FLEE;
exit the tragedy, the tragedy.

Vultures sit and stare,
Vultures everywhere,
Waiting for me, for......me to fall;
waiting for me, to......end it all.

Off in the distance and over the hills,
through the moans, the shrieks, and the shrills;
I hear the soft sounds of the firing squad,
people living and dying......for GOD;
looking for symbols, looking for ways,
yearning for wisdoms of yesterdays.

Vultures sit and stare,
Vultures everywhere,
Waiting for me, for......me to fall;
waiting for me, to......end it all.

a pyramid of love we could never build;
no space is left that broken hearts haven't filled;
the pain gets so bad, and then the tears
for the lost, the forgotten, the wasted years;
but soon after you cry, the pains dissipate,
the mind grows numb and you begin to hate.

Vultures sit and stare,
Vultures everywhere,
Waiting for me, for......me to fall;
waiting for me, to......end it all.

You can try to hide, you can run for cover,
only to crash into the very next lover;
it's one for today and it's one for the road,
to help me get rid of this heavy load;
the gallows are ready and I'm to be hung,
the song of escapade has just been sung.

Everlasting, True, and Strong

An end to all your rules, an end to all your games;
life has nothing good but youthfulness in flames.
An end to perspicacity, an end to solace and sorrow;
life has nothing good but the presence of tomorrow.

At age twenty-four you feel as though
you have lived a lifetime of blues;
but you're barely a third of the way through,
I hate to be the bearer of bad news.

It has been said that nothing lasts forever,
I tell you, that is wrong.
When your heart is made of diamond,
love will always sing its song.

Everlasting, True, and Strong:

It will all come back together,
in love and god and pain;
and when the shadow hits the wall
I tell you, they are all the same.

You say you don't know what to do,
that it can never be the same,
and you are afraid to keep on playing.
After all, love is just a age old game
called, 'Who can stand the rain?'
Yet, it is that pounding crushing rain
that gets you through the door,
and helps you make the flame
burn stronger than before.

Into the City of Death

So give me a hand this time around,
no excuses to be found;
give me a hand this time around.
This is where we take the trip,
we're taking a ride

-

 -

  -

   -

                    we're within the city limits
                              now
                      the city of death.

The Neptune King sees a light
in the eyes of a memory never had.

Let us stick together now,
because let me tell you;
            when you get out there
            howlin'......
            howlin' like a lonely wolf,
you're gonna feel the pain like never before.
The cemetery calls out my name......
            we have a place for you;
the world has stopped and changed direction,
            and love is the reason
            for all the bleedin'......
            hearts.
Relinquish yourself
            from all the pain,
a heart made of stone
            can still break like bone,
            so don't treat love......
            with disdain.

You have to take your chances with love,
just as you must take chances with hate.
The ability to get to the bottom without getting wet,
is a necessary art; let me demonstrate.
You have to stand your ground,
look it square in the face......
      on the question of arrival,
      on the question of growth,
      on the question of climax,
      on the question of forms;
if you try to run from it, if you're afraid to go to the peak,
      then you will be lost.
You must climb the highest point,
      give love a smile......and jump;
You must take strong action.

So many tears have fall-en,
so many years I have tried to es-cape
but the hands of love, they twist around my neck.
A glimpse of the moon perhaps......I should not have seen.
I open up my heart to you.
I open up my heart to you
but no one is calling my name,
it doesn't matter, it's all just the same......
old story of a fool who thinks he has a chance
to win glory.

So many tears have fall-en,
so many years I have tried to es-cape.
Off in the distance a telephone rings,
and outside my window a blackbird sings
his song......so sad;
it makes me feel glad that I'm not the only one.
He is telling me I have one last chance......
to break free.
As the light grows dim and the stars shimmer for awhile;
I guess it's just my imagination
that keeps me smiling,
because there is no other reason at all.

So many tears have fall-en,
so many years I have tried to es-cape
from the road that misery has paved
with my footprints of lead.
I've been over here and I've been over there,
sometimes I get the feeling I've been everywhere
but nowhere at all.
I can't take it anymore,
it makes me so angry.
Oh, where is the pretty girl
to calm the beast within me?

So many tears have fall-en,
so many years I have tried to es-cape,
The dead poet comes to life
bringing with him a razor-sharp knife.
I say, I don't care much for anything,
just a pretty girl;
only she can come close to the dead poet.
Do you know how much he is hurting?
Do you think it is time to concede?
Ask yourself,
is this what you really want, babe,
or is this what you really......need?

Sweet Jeanine

Hey, hey, sweet Jeanine
so delicate, so pristine;
with your submissive stare
and your long, flowing hair;
with your naked pleasing smile
and your heart upon trial;
tell me, how can you be......
tell me, how can you be......
so alone.

With your beautiful sunflower dress
and your soft virginal caress;
with your dark, passionate eyes
and your smooth, velvet thighs;
with your sincere, rainbow tears
and your sensitive, ladylike fears;
tell me, how can you be......
tell me, how can you be......
so alone.

With your innocent, arousing talk
and your cool, seductive walk;
with your radiant, ruby lips
and your hypnotic, hourglass hips;
with your firm sensual bust
and your insatiable teenage lust;
tell me, how can you be......
tell me, how can you be......
so alone.

Love's Final Quest

Flesh to flesh......our visions mesh
in splendid paradise.
For us alone, the bell, it tolls
for the unity of souls, the unity of goals
caught in the grasp of silken thighs;
I rise......
I rise......
caressing ruby hills of symmetry,
lips streaky red, engulfing me;
sturdy and pulsating with no refrain
I reign......
I reign......
until the blessed ooze of infinity
flows through the chasm effortlessly;
such is the glory of love's final quest.
I rest......
I rest......
flesh to flesh......our visions mesh
in splendid paradise.

'Tis Such a Tease

By the touch of a finger, my conscience 'tis stained.
Here, in a teardrop instant of life, I met her,
a native of love from the island of delight;
'twas all so spiritualized,
my mind became inanimate within me.
Below, behind, beneath,
a mother mouse says to her child:

We can never live too long;
when man thought of permanence,
he chose to give himself trouble.
Inventive brains and deep hearts
and years of toil......wasted,
wasted in some hidden, forgotten
corner of the universe;
and I do mean corner, my child.

I have been neglected in this whole affair;
disrespect seems to be the way of the times.
Look at your eyes girl, in the fire,
the warm light mingles
with the cold prosperity.
Oh, hath romance become
a forbidden territory,
ghosts in a fairy-land,
struggle in a struggling world?
You know, I honestly believe in
the ordinary gifts of the storyteller;
but this creature is seldom praised.
If he should possess an unusual share of energy
then he shall lose, lose it to the meek;
for he is a child by nature,
naked with no shields of defense.
In the worst event anyway,
he shall perish with pride.

Below, behind, beneath,
an on looking housefly caught
between a window and a screen
thinks to himself:

We can never live too long;
might not a dreary sleep
be less painful than infinity,
in my position?

I see a hallucinogenic face of hope
with a smile of discouragement;
the haunting impossibility of finding the beautiful girl.
The truth be told, it takes a coincidence of circumstances
one after another, after another.
you may hold a pearl in the palm of your hand
only to watch it disappear with a shimmer,
into the murky waters of fate with no proof
that what you held so close was there, or not there.
So clouds gradually pass, leaving a deep, vivid shade of blue.
Below, behind, beneath,
a hungry spider on the window sill screams:

We can never live too long;
'tis such a tease!
the lonely open ocean,
the clouds shifting in the sky of hope,
the island that lay across the horizon,
the pearl, the beautiful girl,
and the fly before me.

Oh, the cataclysm of a destined future;
life, 'tis such a tease, and such
are the images of summer days.

Thomas Walker

On the Ancient Road of Ruins

Now you only get one heart, when broken there is no repair.
So, step into the cage of hungry lions if you dare,
where no one can avoid the insidious harmful tear
that keeps us twisted
and turnin'......forever after.

You do what you can do, you cheat and you connive,
but nothing can expel the dangers that arrive
on a distant broken shore, a pinch to see if you're alive,
or trapped deep inside
a rustic......hollow dungeon.

So you ask me to tell you which way the wind will blow,
and you ask me to tell you all the secrets that I know,
and you ask me to tell you where I think you'll go
when freedom with open arms
always seems......to forget you.

So you discourage the sun telling him to forget the night,
then you go and tell everyone that you're just expressing your right
to have the same old dream of colliding visions and foresight,
as the doorway keeps getting wider
though you cannot......seem to find it.

But you keep on working harder in hope of getting that promotion,
they kick you when you're down as a test to your devotion,
and every now and then you sip some magic potion,
that makes you wonder
what it is in hell......that everyone is after.

And now that you've been uptown it comes to no surprise
that you don't believe your ears and you can't believe your eyes;
the pretty pictures that surround are nothing but a disguise,
for ambition hides in the flowers
waiting......to destroy you.

Ashes In My Skull

You find yourself so helpless clutched in the jaws of defeat
every time you wake up screaming how your life is so incomplete;
while the morning's golden dew and idle burning heat,
leaves you crawling for angels
that you......don't believe in.

And every now and then on the ancient road of ruins,
you stumble from exhaustion face first into the dunes,
so the next time you blink your eyes impaled with open wounds,
take a look outside
your window......a mistress is calling.

Don't let your heart wither away from a simple lack of tryin',
and don't be afraid to leave the security of a straightened line,
and don't forget that I'm on your side whether or not you're on
mine,
when the war is finally over
and......it's time to surrender.

Mistress Poison

I can see right through your naked eyes,
those wicked little lover lies
but you are my girl / don't ask why girl.
Some things are meant to be
LOST in the emotional conspiracy
and all you can do is offer your solidarity
to release the anxiety.
You see, the love
will disappear / like ripples in a pond
only to come back
with each and every fallen tear,
the tirade and / or the affection,
the echo parade and / or the resurrection.
Oh, mistress poison,
on the broken path to glory,
I'd like to hear your story.
Such fierce adulation / a torch is lit,
and ever so easy, you lead me
to the snake pit of
common safety / the radiant flesh.
You apprehend the reptile
and begin to caress
but you are my girl / don't ask why girl.
Some things are meant to be
LOST in the emotional conspiracy
and all you can do is offer your solidarity
to release the anxiety,
stroking secrets / the fiery waterfall
spurning fortunes / come one, come all.

It's Just a Matter of......TIME!

TIME
the bestial demon
of humanity;
TIME,
always standing in front of and behind
the plans to evade the joyous city.

She's a letter-box version of a hotel queen,
you won't find her name on the walls of the Sistine.
I sit and stare, craving an invitation,
and always accept without hesitation.
There is something about those hungry eyes
that make me come back, in reprise.
Oh, I'll pay anything, anything at all,
to take a walk down that never-ending hall.
Visions of loneliness, visions of you
like tinted glass, the darker side sees through.
The dangers of beauty I cannot elude,
the pleasure of seeing Erato, in the nude.
I will indulge freely whilst I can,
what can possibly stand in the way of my plan?

Yes, you guessed it.

TIME,
so it seems,
the conqueror of all my dreams;
TIME,
that which doth destroy,
all that the heart sets out to employ.

Autumn Love

I've been around town enough to know
that nobody cares where I go;
nobody cares about you or I
or why I'd......die for you.

Maybe I'm just another
lonely, lonely, lonely,
lonely man who doesn't even realize,
that he doesn't need to realize......his fate;
(but I know I want you as my mate)
until the end, until the end.
Can't you see that
love, love, love,
love is a bird that always flies,
it never really dies......forever.
The particles of love may

D   S   E   S
   I   P   R   E

and then,

REALIGN

but they are always there;
they never die, don't despair.

I'll sit here and sing a song for you,
some people do not object, but most do
because it is not happy and it is not new.
But what else is there when you're feeling blue?
When you've got nothing in your pockets but pain;
nothing, nothing in your heart but rain,
and the suicide wheels, they spin in your brain.
What is there to gain, what is there to gain?

Behind the cracks where no one sleeps,
he weeps......for the girl of his dreams;
an equal cosmic glow,
but he just let it slip away,
he just let her go and now......
we will never know.

I offer my heart because that is all I have to give.
I offer my heart because that is all I have to live.
It doesn't matter anyway,
it is the same old thing every day,
no clouds above but the sky is grey.

I am not fast,
but I am not last,
but I am dying.

A little white cat sitting on a fence;
a little white bird says, 'give me six pence
if you want to sit on my post
because I am the bird,
the bird with the most.'
The next thing you know,
the cat swallows the bird,
and all around town everybody has heard
about the annual love fest
down on west pussy lane.
The word is that the chicks there
make the blood rush through your veins,
and then the rains......come,
and then the rains......come,
and then the rains......come,
and then the rains......come,
gushing from your head.

What would you think my darling,
if I wandered through your garden
telling people, 'don't despair,
for she has black flowers in her hair?'

Thomas Walker

Everybody's intrusive......when your down,
everybody's abusive......when your down.
Everybody's haunting......when your down,
everybody's taunting......when your down.
Everybody's grateful......when your down,
everybody's hateful......when your down.
Everybody's confused......when your down,
everybody's amused......when your down.
Everybody's annoying......when your down,
everybody's destroying......when your down.
Everybody's smiling......when your down,
everybody's beguiling......when your down.
Everybody's lying......when your down,
everybody's dying......when your down.

I wish I could have slowed things down,
it has all blown by so fast.
I doubt I will ever see her again,
I should have known it wouldn't last,

and that bitter memory hurts me so,
it cuts right through the bone.
Now life just lingers on and on,
for not making her my own.

Some say that love just brings pain,
and that the good
never outweighs the bad.
Honey, that is where they are always wrong
because nothing could ever outweigh
the good times that we've had.

I love you
softer than eternity
but I had my chance,
now the romance
blows by like a
cool autumn breeze.

Ashes In My Skull

That last night, I whispered in your ear,
wondering, wondering if you could hear:

Oh if I had but one wish
I would give that wish to you
to use for wealth, health, power, fame,
or for whatever you wanted to;
and if you should use that wish
to forever rid of me
then at least I would know
that I left passionately.
For the king without the queen of spades
slashes his wrists with razor blades.

And like the leaves on the trees,
it is those little subtleties
that make us fall......
fall in and out of love.

Violet Summer

I don't know how I'm going to tell you,
I do not care anymore.
It all happened as I expected,
just like the time before.
I don't know if it is you,
or someone rapping at my door.
I'd throw it all away and leave,
the untimely forgotten lore.
Somehow I am still thinking
about the night we went for a drive;
recollection of a melody,
'five to one, one in five'.
I don't know if it ever happened,
we were barely alive,
but the next time we sail that gloomy ocean
let's step outside and take a dive.

I have to
give some(body)
my love;
if you don't want it,
I will go......
find some(body)
who will
take it and show......
me that it is true
that you get back
all (you give).

Everything that we know of
seems to find a way to die;
I say yesterday is just a nightmare
and all you can do is cry.
Every memory is made of tiny colors,
won't you look me in the eye;

can you see the violet summer
of the year I taught you to fly?
And what a time, what a time,
the time of our first flight;
sitting naked on mushroom pillows
and playing with the light.
Images of shining flowers
made for pretty dreams that night;
yeah, I've put that little episode
on the side of life that went all right.

I have to
give some(body)
my love;
if you don't want it,
I will go......
find some(body)
who will
take it and show......
me that it is true
that you get back
all (you give).

Thomas Walker

The Girl of His Dreams

He is a boy that gets bored with conversation,
he needs a fix from the girl machine.
She is a girl of quiet desperation,
she hears a voice but she doesn't respond.
He is a boy of intense annihilation,
he lost his heart at the age of ten.
She is a girl who lives in moderation,
she only needs her world filled with love.
He is a boy without a destination,
he can't find anything worth fighting for.
She is a girl of radiant inspiration,
she is passion's muse from day to day.
He is a boy of extreme intoxication,
he gets high off of a gentle touch.
She is a girl without inhibition,
she does whatever she feels is right.
He is a boy who works hard for aggravation,
he gets paid in fool's gold by the pimps of life.
She is a girl of intimate insatiation,
she needs to make love every day.
He is a boy of similar aspiration,
he wants to satisfy her every night.
She is a girl who gets torn by infatuation,
she needs a boy who won't let her down.
He is a boy who reveals his dedication,
he is not afraid to recognize her needs.
She is a girl who can't handle separation,
she needs her love to last forever.
He is a boy with a vivid imagination,
he thinks that he'll find the girl of his dreams.

Feelin' Like a Whale

Somehow, at twenty-five,
I feel so......old.
I somehow pray,
as I float away in my bed.
I pray that this delirious thought
will soon leave my head;
pray meaning to request in a humble manner,
just simple rhetoric with emotion, of course.
What would something be without emotion?
It would just be......something,
just another battle over nothing.

I'm sorry I do not feel that way,
for every nothing......is something.
Even a rock has feeling
lying on the ground or rolling down the river.
So the next time
I fall in love
won't you take me for a ride,
because,
I'm never thinking too straight
when I'm feelin' satisfied,
and you'll never know
how I feel when I'm low,
and right now I'm really low.

I've never been so alone,
nobody loves me anymore,
and why does the whale
so often drift ashore?

Fly Down to Mexico

Another absent mind in a progressing world,
another bullet fired, another body hurled.
Ennui, so bored.
Ennui, so bored.

I don't want to do anything with anybody but you
but there is always some obligation,
something we have to do.

I'm such a loser, life isn't worth a thing;
a psychotic abuser, pain is all I bring.
Reckless memory get away from meeeeee!

Go to your little masquerade.
I use to go as a human
dreaming of a place (a secret place).
Now I go as nothing (just in case).
Born on the ground in the dust,
a revolutionary in the underworld of trust.
I might die, I must
but it isn't important (really)
for a long, long time the ground was covered;
for a long, long time on top we hovered.

Yet unsuspecting memories,
they creep up from behind
and pull you down below
to remind us (of a time) of
magic potions;
intimate lotions
on soft, young, beautiful skin.
A day of love, a day of love,
another day of love......without pain.
The strange cold white, far away light
is barely in sight.

The passion is in the sky and wind,
the passion is in the backbone of night.
The power of gods and goddesses
some of violence, some benign,
lies in hopelessness and despair,
a re-awakening;
I am finished, life is finished,
life is not fun anymore.
There are not many second chances with life
and if you quit you will never wonder.

Praise the destitute, praise me.
(I better hurry, I've got five minutes to catch my plane)
I'm ready to go flying, I'm ready to be free.
Perhaps solitude is not the answer?
It will take you down quick, kind of like cancer.

I know that this is not the way to get through to you
but I never know what to say, what else can I do.
I have no feelings anymore, for any life or any death around
but darling, I do surely know that you're something to be found.
You're something to be found.
You're something to be found.

(In My Head)

There's a pillow riding
'neath my eye,
(in my head)
and a little machine
who knows where I've been
(in my head)
is climbing the walls
of telemetry
(in my head).
An echoing voice says,
can this all be
(in my head)
just a penitentiary
of daylight
(in my head)
latched around
her hips......
(in my head)
hobbling over to close
innocent curtains
(in my head)?
My safety lies
in a delicate bed.

Everywhere a Peach

How many tears must I run through the gutters
before I get to fly so high?
The uncontrolled insolence has me down
and ablaze are the ubiquitous,
the curse of the countryside.

But first, one must suffer the triumphant blows
of destined limits;
to breathe and die as a great poet would,
in the Isolated Palace.

The heart is a heavy thing you know,
that which lifts the WOMAN;
alas, a feast of scholarly beauty;
I think I see a light burning out
in the city of Musa.

There they build nothing but promises,
breeding mortal goddesses;
such tasty lust, I have desired to go there.
I may not understand why,
but I still love the sweet Mother of Cupid;
yet I weep for no deaths she may cause.

In a useless daze, roused by wine
such an evil lamp is lit
for one lover who wants two.
So, we drop like fruit from a tree,
to rot......or forever be uplifted
by each days growing.
My fate depends on the RAIN.

God Writes a Poem

In the midnight pub,
the real lonely hearts club,
even God writes a poem or two,
the way he always wanted to
but how could he ever compare
to the man in the blue chair.

He tips his hat to the Neptune King,
sitting at the end of the bar.

God says to him, "You know,
sometimes I wish that I was
a poet in the seventeenth century."

The Neptune King replies,
"I never bring up the powers that you use,
so don't you tell me
how to write the blues."

When I Write in the Wind

Do not worry,
have no fear,
because when I write in the wind
an emotional frenzy is pinned

......to entertain,
......to nurture,
......to increase,
......to give,
......to manifest,
......to acquire,

and the lady that you once knew
has left you stricken with the flu
......of misanthropy.

The forgotten chores,
the cheap dime stores,
the zealous bores,
the polluted shores,
the street-side whores,
behind locked doors.
Is it mine or yours?
When it rains it pours,
the butterfly roars
and everyone ignores
......the gist of it.

Do not worry, have no fear,
because if it's kindness you refuse
then your misery is your muse.
Now people just bring you down
to the poets lost in the town
......of misanthropy.

A pessimistic clown
hiding behind a frown.
Did you make it uptown?
If you don't swim you'll drown.
Lonely girl in a wedding gown,
don't fall facedown;
listen to the soft sundown
with eyes, sad and brown.
Don't look up or down
or you'll end up in a showdown
......with destiny.

Do not worry,
have no fear,
because if you never ever find
the one who'll treat you so kind,
then you can come swim with me
through the dark, darkened sea
......of misanthropy.

Did you pay your bill?
Did you write a will?
Did you get your fill
from the golden drill?
Are you on the pill?
Did you get your thrill
from taking a spill
with the fool on the hill,
while I'm out on a sill
knowing the next step will
......kill me.

Do not worry,
have no fear,
because repetition is the key
to infinite reality.
Just like the poet and the muse
are together the bomb and fuse
......of misanthropy.

It is on the rise,
I can see it in your eyes;
the lover's demise.
You've got to be wise
and just improvise,
tell me white lies;
a politician in disguise.
You'll get your prize,
don't ever compromise
what happiness buys
......for you.

Do not worry, have no fear,
because you'll get back all you give
if you should chose to live;
for the prediction of the soothsayers
is that emptiness gets frozen in layers
......of misanthropy.

Which One......is Yours

Put on a mask and say, "I love you."
Put on a mask and say, "I hate you,
I want to kill you, I can kill anyone."

To you, I rebel, and to me I just see
a little bit different than thee,
and there's a hole in my heart where the love disappears,
and there's a place in my head where the hate adheres.

Individuality lay crushed beneath the wings of conformity.
Be one with us, be one with us, give in to us,
and with non-conformity now a convention itself,
what remains?

So, what if I choose to kiss Lady Death right on the lips?
If you let me be me, I'll let you be you.
We'll talk, we'll laugh.......
now I'm like you, just like me;
waiting around for felicity,
waiting around with tenacity.
No longer will I run, I've got a gun
I am not afraid of death, better hold your breath......
before you try to say that one.

Everyone has got railroad ties in their brain.
The problem is that there usually is not a train,
just a little bit of pleasure, a lot of pain,
and that is......insane.

How many times must I say, 'good bye my love'
before you'll say, 'please don't go'?

No future beholds me now.
Oh, that gloomy feeling, that melancholic nightmare
driving me out, away from the sky.

A poet's paradise sure is nice.
There, you will find what you want to find
because I found what I found......life.
A life that has been so much better at times.
I say, 'life cannot get much worse than today,'
but tomorrow,
I say, 'life cannot get much worse than today,'
but tomorrow,
I say, 'life cannot get much worse than today,'
but tomorrow,
I say, 'life cannot get much worse than today.'
A steady line,
down,
    down,
        down,
            down,
                down,
                    deep below.

What cavernous hell have I run into now?
Everybody wants some time away
from these cavernous pits, if just for a day.
Are you afraid of the man in the long black coat;
afraid that he'll build a moat......around your dreams?

I try to understand but you won't take my hand,
you don't care how I feel.
You just spit in my face and say my poetry sucks.
You wouldn't give me two bucks
for a book of my rhymes and passion.
But here, I grow everyday......in a very strange way.
Now, I have more than one heart.
There's one heart to live,
there's one heart to give,
and a room full of hearts to break.

In the Aftermath

Guiding my ship into the narrow confines
of life's mysterious canal,
I find myself......here on Earth;
tuning into the channel of love,
giving a little push, and giving a little shove.
A planet obsessed with battle,
the nature of quagmires.
Firing my weapon, atomic particles explode;
remnants of me......to the power of infinity.
The conflict becomes ephemeral
and backing out......I leave the Milky Way behind,
a reckless sea of abandon, in search of a new enemy.

I am not complaining about where I've been
I am not complaining about the state I'm in;
the present and the past, lying, dying,
or the future that is cast.
I am not complaining about who I'm with
or why I live, the love I have,
or don't have to give.
I am not complaining about the weather;
whether or not I will succeed in the end.

But, who was it that lied to me?

Love and live, live and love?
It is a little sequence bearing down on me,
and who am I, to tell you what to see?
I see......softly falling rain;
then you don't need me, if you don't love me.

A Poet Always has a Gun

About the end; hear no more.
      Are you stuck pondering move one?
About the end; fear no more.
      Fuck the earth, there still is sun.
      Brother go, and get your gun,
      there is no where left to run.
      Without your friends you'll have no fun.
      Fuck them all, you've got a gun.

      Tomorrow's pain is now undone.
        Undone........
        yeah,
        undone.

About the end; hear no more.
Boy, can't you handle the weight?
About the end; fear no more.
      Isn't it all just a simple twist of fate?
      No turning back, it's too damned late,
      you're on the other side of the gate.
The poet is in an altered state,
the game is over, you took the bait,

      and doesn't it make you so irate?
        Irate........
        yeah,
        irate.

She said, "You know, not everyone
speaks of suicide, you're such a pessimist.
Who wants you?"

I said, "You know, not everyone
notices my eyes, or that I'm just a visionary realist
who wants you!"

Love is nothing at all.
Slap your face and bury your heart.
Love is nothing at all
yet......it takes nothing at all
to make you cry in the dark.
The good times with our backs against the wall
always seem to make us fall.
The good times, the good times,
always seem so hard to recall.
Love truly is, nothing at all.

Everyone get a stone......go ahead and get a stone,
everyone get a stone......go ahead and shower me with stones.

In the valley of gloom
down by the garden of doom,
the lonely howl at the moon.
I will meet you on the other side
with an ounce of pride buried deep inside.
Dancing in the sunrise, everybody dies
with eternity in their lips and eyes.
A labyrinth of days were set ablaze by the sun's rays.
Now that it's done, and thanks to no one,
I'm just another savage with a gun.

If only we did not think,
we would not think about happiness.
Count to ten, say it again.
If only we did not think,
we would not think about happiness.
The truth be told, Calliope cannot hear us
as time evaporates the private paradise,
(our dreams) the wickedness of amenity.
We advance from 'the broken committee'
at midnight in the city......of Death.
The death of nothing I care to believe in.
The essence of gold......
to copulate, to populate,
to save another soul.

Let the trumpets of solitude play for me,
a sad tyrant in a land of love;
without a smile, without a smile,
a little guile never hurts the King.
See him sing
without a smile, without a smile.
How loud the trumpets can be
for virility;
uncontrollable grotesque obscenity,
there is no one like me.
How loud the trumpets can be.

It is the reason you ask, that is the reason why
I must sigh......in madness and in violence,
and then silence.
Shake your head and say, "I don't know,
I guess I'd rather be dead, real dead."
What I have in store for you is a special treat;
but you cannot tell anyone, it involves a gun.

You cannot allow people to go,
you cannot allow people to grow.
It is a never ending game, a crying shame
if everybody is late for 'the show'
so......I ask myself what is wrong?

What's wrong with this spiral connection I'm a-dreamin'?
What's wrong with this evil resurrection I'm a-schemin'?
What's wrong with this naked direction I'm a feelin'?
What's wrong with this broken affection I'm a-healin"?
What's wrong with this unknown projection I'm a-livin'?
What's wrong with this deadly infection I'm a-givin'?

Is there anyone,
anyone.......that can see where I'm a-comin' from?
Is there anyone,
anyone......who would like to borrow my gun?

Pyramid of Love

A woman builds a pyramid in a man's heart;
the stones arrive one by one, each stone arises with:

Every smile......a stone.
Every 'I love you'......a stone.
Every passionate kiss......a stone.
Every cry on the shoulder......a stone.
Every time we laugh together......a stone.
Every erotic love-making episode......a stone.

Higher and higher the pyramid rises,
a tomb of love!
When the love dies, we start anew.
A new pharaoh in the land of love,
the construction of a new pyramid begins
with all of your treasures (memories)
locked inside for the next life.
Do you want one great pyramid
or several smaller ones?
The base determines the height,
you must know what is right for you;
for some are never completed,
others, finished too soon!
So, be smart and think it over.
Plan it out first,
because when you put the last stone
on a great pyramid
it becomes......forever!

Down by the Waterfront

"Lonely people feed the stars,"
he told me, like a strange character
from wonderland;
"I am no dormouse," he muttered to himself,
"I am the Fire-eating Mole,
so put that head back on my bookshelf."
He could not understand a word I spoke.
he screamed, "you are all slimy slaves!"
and then I awoke.

It was a rainy day when I found a letter drift ashore:

Hello, how are you
my friend without fears;
come and take what is yours
before the rain clears.
I miss your sensitive ears.
From, the one you adore!

It is peculiar, none the less,
how love leaves you
stranded on an island waiting for more,
waiting......always waiting for more.
Lately, I have been thinking too much
about being in love.
I think about laughing,
the warmth of passionate eyes
locking on to each other,
and speaking in geometric patterns
too intense to measure.
The forgetfulness of pleasure in
the form of a smile that is real,
the form of a touch that is real,
the form of a kiss that is real
the form of a seduction that is real.

One has to be brave to believe in love
and no one is more brave than the poet,
spilling his insides for everyone to see
while all the rest hide behind a veneer.
So pretty with ribbons in their hair,
so safe with crosses around their necks.

It is much easier to live
with the protection of a shield
but the poet,
expressing himself ever so freely,
becomes vulnerable.
Vulnerable to the disease of pain;
and love is a vulnerable emotion,
a true sign of bravery.
So make way for the new age gunslinger
who strolls into town
fearing no one, nothing.

Can't you hear me screaming madly?
Can't you see me strolling blindly?
"No, not really" she said.
Down by the waterfront
my heart f
        e
        l
          l as I tried to flee;
no sense hanging around beneath
this blackened sea...... waiting
for consolidation......with you.
Can't you feel my heart burning?
"No, not really" she said.

Was it just another dream
or hath my mind played tricks
on me once again,
fooled into thinking that perhaps
the Other World is real,
and This World is just a dream?

Ashes In My Skull

When you awake, for the sake of Mr. Mole.....
mark this spot in my brain, this partial fantasy.
There is no dream, just endless sleep.
"Mr. Mole, why are my eyes frozen?"

"Why are you so concerned......
with the removal of ashes in my skull?"

Oh, I am awake again to tell
another lonesome story.
I came to kill a bird I knew,
whose quoth I felt was so untrue......

"A-sing, sing, singin'
a melody of hate;
puts the little black bird
in an unconscious state."

"A-chop, chop, choppin',
his head falls to the floor;
taken into context,
nevermore is nevermore."

And on this volatile high, I strip the world
free of madness one last time.
Sunny days and flowers in a vase,
all for you, you know it was always for you.

Butterfly Revelry

Would you like to sing my song?
Would you like to - - - - - - - - oh, yeah;
all night long?

Would you like to run my life?
Would you like to - - - - - - - - oh, yeah;
be my wife?

Would you like to be my girl?
Would you like to - - - - - - - - oh, yeah;
wear my pearl?

Long, long blonde hair rolling across her breasts;
Satan's daughter is hoping to be blessed
with flying specs of butterfly revelry;
three times a night is all right by me.
Let us get together, don't you hesitate.
Never is never, it is never too late!
Never is never, it is never too late!
Never is never, it is never too late!

THERE

Eating human flesh,
and breaking through
an embryonic sack
to swallow some loins,
larger ones first.
All the while,
the meek stay in the back
......only watching,
but they are THERE.

And,
THERE is no universe.
THERE is no poetry (stuck somewhere in between).
THERE is no isolation.

Yet,
THERE is sex.
THERE is a warm
and wet vagina awaiting
......to engulf
a thick hard penis.

I know it is only my opinion,
but if it is your penis
and her vagina,
then you are stuck
somewhere in between.
If not, you are
on the outside looking in.

Offspring of Her Frailty

On her pedestal of shame she rekindles
a previous relationship, a dying fire;
a fallen woman thinks sacred of them all......
and I, holding the key to her silence,
will vanish out of life completely.

Somehow, someway, somewhere......
I will go back and meet her again;
yet, I will have no heart,
thought will cease from the start,
and I will be without the misery
of knowing what might have been.

But for now I cannot erase
the inevitable fate of the ace......
of spades that I hold in my hand,
the one that I found in the sand
on the shores of the lonely lover's sea.

I sailed through the night,
I fought the dim light......
that crept into the back of my brain.
A little bit of love translates
to a whole lot of pain,
and I have seen my share of pain.

So every now and then,
you'll work your way back again;
back on my troubled mind
until the Princess of passion decides,
I find another hurting kind.

The Emperor Mouse

......and the
Emperor Mouse
said,
I tell you this......
I can sing so high,
I can sanctify
all forms of hate.

Let me demonstrate
the uncommon
fate......
of my foe.

You see, I know
about the Lions
on the other side
of my door,
so I do not
go outside
anymore.

I do not need
the strife
of running
for my life,
for I am
the
Emperor Mouse.

Venus in her Eyes

You know that I see you
      through fragile-like mirrors.
You know that I see you
      when troubles arise.
I know we could make it
      in gardens of Eden.
I know when I see Venus
      deep in your eyes.

With her Picasso stories and her lipstick dreams;
with her speak-no-evil lies and her suicide schemes.

She looks for the Devil as if she could not care less;
then her silk covered heart tears like her dress.

She comes to the master of dark, lurid visions;
she comes to hide out from the fatal collisions.

But the intensity of her love is turned up a degree;
and the plot thickens with each visit to me.

You know that I see you
      through fragile-like mirrors.
You know that I see you
      when troubles arise.
I know we could make it
      in gardens of Eden.
I know when I see Venus
      deep in your eyes.

The Implicite

2 to 4......I remember it well.
The Implicite was the 16th customer of St. Mary.
Call me Marie, she said......I'm dead,
you're dead and we are all wise here.
Call me Marie. she said......I'm dead.
Oh, and by the way, who are you?
Well my lady,
I am the Implicite......196 days a year.
Excuse me, there is a white horse
dancing in my eyes,
he has springs on his heels,
neighing, you must know good how it feels......
to be deep inside......a fantasy.

Wandering around discreetly......the night wind,
whirling with passion, speaks to the Implicite.
My book is white, transparent white,
but it once was red, blood red.
In the golden age of the Implicite
the night could never close my book.
So what do you mean, your dead?

Insanity's flower blossoms in the rain,
crystal clear, no inside or out.
Come closer, Mr. Nobody.
Come closer......
and smell the fragrance of promise;
the Implicite knows what it's all about.
The story of a life......Intent and Actuality;
protagonist and antagonist, the roles reverse,
never intending to meet face to face.
For actuality is just a shadow,
an image cast upon the mind
by blocking the rays of perception......
waiting to waste just a little more time.

Time is yours and mine is yours to waste;
until the Implicite is erased, encased
in a plaster mould for all to see.
A tragedy is told......'Everything is Sold!'

The poet hides in the last vacant room;
the mat by the door says, WELCOME......to doom!
Desperately, silence whispers in the air,
The butterfly screams......Marie is dead! Marie is dead!
Mourning, weeping, stormy void;
the Implicite, conqueror of dreams, is off to bed.

Morning, weeping, stormy void;
the lizard's wife goes out
to try on her newest shade of green.
The truth is she'd rather not be seen.
The miracle man cast humanity some shade;
nothing really matters as long as he gets paid,
or laid......in the halls by Faith.
The sky pilot, hostility, plundering space;
never knowing what to look for......just finish the race.
It is time to pull out the ace......
of spades, the Implicite card.

Into the forest where the mockingbird sings loud,
the ladies with the biggest diamonds are proud.
Pride and prowess, wicked ways;
sing, sing they will do anything,
anything if you pull on the right string.
The Implicite knows......for he is King.

Down below, what does all of this mean?
A flag waving free that your eyes cannot see;
just sea......deep green and shadowy blue.
The machine made machine
fights to decide what belongs to who.
If you feel as though there is nothing you can do;
wait until the sun drifts out of sight,
the whole world will be left......for the Implicite.

Ashes In My Skull

Everyone questions the way that you live,
but no one will give......a smile to the dead;
so go ahead and do what you want.
Get what you can get, indulge full measure;
dig what you can dig, whatever your treasure.
For there are no wrongs, no rights,
when it comes to pleasure.

Fallen in and drifting out, nothing left to dream about.
No hype, no hate, nothing left to desecrate.
I can see you standing there just like me,
the forest tree......standing in the rain, ignoring the pain.
Everyone is insane, except you, me......and the Implicite.

Committee of Fools

We are just a poor lonesome committee of fools,
singing about delusion, breaking all the rules.
We have nowhere to go, we have nothing to do,
we are higher than high, don't misconstrue.

We are just a poor lonesome committee of fools
in the company of pragmatists, trained in the schools.
Up on the television stand, a picture of the world
locked up in a battle of sapphire and emerald.

We are just a poor lonesome committee of fools,
looking for every pretty girl, lost in life's duel.
Out in the alleyway, the mad poet in disguise
asks you if it's funny, how fast the time flies.

We are just a poor lonesome committee of fools,
with classic double vision wrapped up in spools.
Over at the shorelines, silky seductive thighs,
and heads bobbing forward; peering passion eyes.

We are just a poor lonesome committee of fools,
climbing up beanstalks looking for the jewels.
Destroying the palace of the sullen sky kings;
never afraid to fly too high, even with wax wings.

The Next Place

The next place, is a place of Wanton.
The intricacy of an opinion
which suffers in the mind;
how often are we incapable of
        travel,
a motive of corruption begun to
        unravel.

I cannot learn as I read.
I cannot learn as I observe.
I cannot learn as I speak.
I cannot learn by virtue.
I cannot learn by honor.
I cannot learn by truth.
I can only learn by the confidence
      ......of knowing.
We are all subject to bundles of information;
information which we will categorize
       in our own place
       (the next place).

I hear some Utopian scream of exception,
and some new-fangled way of conception.
I hear a dialect altered each day,
       but must confess
that each word is a conviction of reality,
       the nakedness or truth,
       the nakedness of feeling.

Infinite images may be drawn from a word
by a scheming visionary.
       Forever.

Strings

Oooh - - - - - - - - - - oooh
hey, hey, I've gotta go now, babe.
I've been trying to tell you about the little things,
like going insane and the pain that it brings,
and people afraid to let go of the strings
tied to the back of their
          notion;
tied to the back of their
          ocean of paaaa - - - - - - in.

Oooh - - - - - - - - - - oooh
hey, hey, I've gotta go now, babe.
These freight train memories are dragging me down.
I have to do whatever it takes to get rid of this frown,
even if it means taking a trip to the town
where everyone sings a
          song;
where everyone sings
          along in paaaa - - - - - - in.

Oooh - - - - - - - - - - oooh
hey, hey, I've gotta go now, babe.
I know what it is that you have to say to me
about the howling wind and the burning sea,
and leaving my mind stained with the misery
of taking too much without
          giving;
of taking too much without
          living in paaaa - - - - - - in.

An Evening to Look Forward to

Two make love
in an impassioned
frenzy;
swimming
nakedness
in a
backyard pool
every evening
after school.

Fires to the right,
fantasia to the left;
one wave
and
you're enthralled,
another
and
your bereft.

Shooting
everywhere
is a hot
liquid nightmare,
the fortuitous
event.

......if I only had the time

Everyone is the same to me,
the fire and the ice;
just another wave away,
from the gates of paradise.

To every composer of the blues
and everyone singing happy news.
To every girl who's caught my eyes
and everyone who's criticized......me.

To every little piggy in town
and everyone who's put me down.
To every girl who is conceding
and everyone who's misleading......me.

To every maker of calamity
and everyone imprisoned by humanity.
To every girl who has walked away
and everyone who's tried to betray......me.

Oh, I'd kill you all tomorrow
but I haven't got the time.
Yes, I'd kill you all tomorrow
but I haven't got the ......time!

To every teacher of conform
and everyone sheltered from the storm.
To every girl I have reinstated
and everyone who's hated......me.

To every soldier out to even the score
and everyone against the universal war.
To every girl who is just a tease
and everyone who's tried to please......me.

To every queen in wonderland
and everyone waiting, head in hand.
To every girl up on the gallows
and everyone who hallows......me.

Oh, I'd kill you all tomorrow
but I haven't got the time.
Yes, I'd kill you all tomorrow
but I haven't got the ......time!

To every minister of slaughter
and everyone walking on water.
To every girl who has left me alone
and everyone who's tried to own......me.

To every innocent man on the run
and everyone clinging to their gun.
To every girl who's brought me tears
and everyone who fears......me.

To every father/mother of confusion
and everyone with grandeurs of delusion.
To every girl of the sunny skies
and everyone who denies......me.

Oh, I'd kill you all tomorrow
but I haven't got the time.
Yes, I'd kill you all tomorrow
but I haven't got the ......time!

(the common orchid is not common)

In the midst of a rhyme,
most of the time I'm, I'm,
I'm dried up and
      runnin' a-way,
      runnin' a-way
from the flowering temptation
of my satiation. I'm, I'm,
I'm losing my petals and
      dyin' to-day,
      dyin' to-day.
Oh, girl on the moon,
I'll be home soon. I'm, I'm,
I'm in love with you and
      goin' crazy,
      goin' crazy.
Give me a place to hide,
give me a place to hide;
      a garden of gloom,
      in a valley of doom.
Give me a place to hide,
give me a place to hide
      from all that deride......
      upon me.

bird that's chirpin'
girl who's flirtin'
blood that's squirtin'
heart that's hurtin'
earth that's shakin'
girl who's fakin'
head that's achin'
heart that's breakin'
love that's heatin'
vulture that's eatin'

slower…slower…slower…slower……

Give me a place to hide,
give me a place to hide
      from all that deride……
      upon me.

Time bombs, silver dollars, a darkened room, and stress;
one liners, sad stories, the jack of hearts,
      Cinderella had to confess:
      How all those go together you'll just have to guess.
      Those who are happy do not need to impress.

Lust in a bottle, whispering, cherry lips so endless;
black satin, white lace, life in a bed,
      Casanova had to confess:
      If you want me to love you, you'll have to undress.
      Those who are happy do not need to impress.

Creed, crosses, deadly sins, a virgin prayer with finesse;
retribution, sacrifice, your abstinence,
      St. Anthony had to confess:
      If you want my help, you'll have to say, God bless.
      Those who are happy do not need to impress.

Elevators, traffic jams, white shirts, starched and pressed;
chemical wars, polluted shores, education,
      the Ape had to confess:
      If you want to be like me, you'll have to regress.
      Those who are happy do not need to impress.

chasers of the GOLDen girl

You say that you would like to meet the devil,
but you are afraid to play with fire.
You say that you would like to sell your soul,
but you cannot sell anything without a buyer.
Hey, hey, Alice,
please say it isn't so.
Pray for me, Alice,
at least you can make yourself grow.
Hey, hey, little pearl-eyed queen
don't look down, the sky is green.
Isn't it strange how every day seems
like another wall built around your dreams.

I heard the roar of the crowd as the blood started falling.
Is someone calling me?
I slept right through the winter's violent storms;
shapes and forms of things to be.
Do you ever wake up screaming,
from dreaming bits and pieces of agony?
Dreams of loveliness, naked conceit;
you can't beat the girl I met last night.
Woke up today to start the new year,
had a beer and cursed the morning light.
I sure do wish that I had not awaken,
it has taken her out of my sight.

Don't always believe what you are told.
One man's penny is another man's GOLD;
just like some choose to stay in the game,
while others decide to fold.

The days I have spent
running around looking for an angel,
were a waste of time because every girl out there
is coming straight from hell.

Ashes In My Skull

Those sensual fantasies in the elusive corridor,
see you crawling across the floor.
Aquatic dreams and a limit to your life;
no signs aboard this cargo ship.
You are ready when you're ready,
when you are ready for the trip.

Everybody out there lined up from dark to bright.
You'll see it when you see it, when you see it at night;
and the consequences mortify the chasers of the GOLD.
You realize when you realize, when you realize you're old.

And who are you to whisper to me,
"what's your name and your fantasy?"
Look for me in the middle of June,
I'll be singing along to a different tune:
Ode to the Love that Brought me Hatred.
Gallons of erotic joy gone to waste,
but not a moment in haste,
and it is all right if you don't like me.

Let us rid of all the days,
All of the numbers, they are so depressing;
the end of the week, the end of the month,
the end of the year, let me rid of them all.
Let life be one long continuum with no end,
on and on, on and on, on and on, on and on.
Let us work all the time, all day, every day.
Take away the weekend; let us be who we really are.
Let us be enslaved with nothing to look forward to
but nothing to pass us by, like a tease.

Maker of Misconception

She went down slowly,
taking life inch by inch;
you never know what you're getting into,
said the lion to the finch.

When things are going great
you're afraid to lose control,
but in the very same instant
you would sell your only soul.

He built his pyramids up so high,
but all civilizations must fall;
he came home screaming madly,
why do I even come home at all.

She unzipped her dress,
thinking exactly just the same;
it is the maker of misconception
that causes all of the pain.

We,
we never really made love;
we just kind of passed the time.
I,
I needed you so much;
I just didn't know what to do.
You,
you tore open my heart;
you just had to get it out.
Now I don't care,
so you don't care,
because I don't care,
because you don't care.

Brittle Leaf on a Dead Black Rose

I've been thinking about
a dead black rose,
and what it has meant.
I've been thinking about
the way love comes and goes,
and why it causes lament.

I gave some love
      I should've kept;
I kept some love
      I should've gave;
and now I am here, where I belong;
nothing right but nothing wrong
         except......
I feel like I'm living at the bottom
      of a grave!
Here I am again......
        no one in sight,
        no one in sight,
        no one in sight..
Here I am, alone again, here I am alone;
looking up I see the sky, now that I'm on my own.

More than 400 years ago,
400 years ago my friend,
people were walking, talking, stalking,
and thinking about the end.
What are you supposed to do?
Answer me in the dark.
Answer me in the dark, that is all I ask.
Because the 8th mask is the best
for it is the mask, the mask of rest!

Anxiety is a God,
to all those who cannot wait;

you have to see,
you have to see,
you have to see.
What are you supposed to do?
She's just another girl
to whom I could've given so much love;
but things never seem to work out
when forever is a black rose,
and the moon softly glows
across my dim-lit ocean.

Red lights glaring in columns, as I head between......
a door......a force......a spirit within......
guides me to the next one,
so I can give my all to YOU.
Every, every bit of it;
all that I have, but nothing at all.
Pray for me and the girl who is just a dream;
let me die by her side.

In love, we always suspect there is only sex;
and in sex, we always wish there was love;
the two converge into a desperate scream;
just another painting, just another death.

RED - - - - - BLACK - - - - - WHITE

(Black)......
        the darkened universe,
        the evil always present.
Present......
        the little bit of light,
        the little bit of (white).
And (red)......
        the gleam of her eyes,
        the gleam of her lips,
        the gleam of her heart;
        all that there is to live for
        amidst the black and white!

Making love is making hate,
every time you make me wait
for that special moment in the sun.

What would you think if I told you,
that I've never been so unhappy in all my life,
but still, I want you as my wife?
Would you walk out on me to look anew;
or would you fight and struggle to wash away
the Neptune blue?
What would you do?

Ask me if I've ever been happy......
I'll say sure everyone has their moment,
      free from sorrow,
        though......'tis always brief.
Ask me when I was the happiest......
I'll say each and every time that you said,
      you loved me,
        though......'tis just a leaf.

Sunflower Tears

The luxuries of languish,
sleeping in my bed in anguish;
a double vision confrontation,
potent sexual integration;
yet how can I be sure that they are,
with this portable seduction in a jar.
The bittersweet taste of their pleasure,
one more time for full measure;
between the legs of solitude,
starry eruption, you cannot elude;
overflowing chasms, so humid, so hot,
so many have come to this sacred spot;
lolled by the hush of the naked twilight,
to compose unity's song all through the night.

I miss those days of lascivious fun,
but now my life is coming undone;
I just don't need any sunflower tears'
the emptiness of wasted years;
another lurid aurora blunder,
makes me lay in bed and wonder.
Through my head, memories creep,
miserable midnight liquid sleep;
frivolous transfer of a vast mind,
infused with pain for some to find;
ecstasy hearts of flexible glass,
every evening comes, to pass;
young lovers wrapped in the heat of lust,
down their road, bricks turn to dust.

Reptilian Conquest

Just when you thought
that you had it all figured out,
infinity sheds its skin,
and leaves you sitting here again......
in doubt.

Neptune my friend,
there's no need to pretend,
won't you take me to the end;
down
down
down
to the bottom of the sea.
I'll crawl inside a shell.
I know you might think it's hell,
but at least I'll be rid of the misery.
Oh yeah, oh yeah,
you know what I'm talking about.

But to my surprise
I still hear the cries,
lights still shine into my eyes;
down
down
down
far and frozen deep below.
There's no use trying to escape,
the monster is loose, and has to rape.
Melting water must always flow.
Oh no, oh no,
you know what I'm talking about.

I am sitting here on my window sill
thinking I'm very, very ill,
but I'll just take another pill;

down
down
down
let my worries blow away
for a while, while I smile,
everyone likes to smile for awhile.
Anxiety for the sacred lay.
Oh yeah, oh yeah,
you know what I'm talking about.

Just when you thought
that you had it all figured out;
infinity sheds its skin
and leaves you sitting here again......
in doubt.

I should have left, but I stayed
alone, alone with destiny's maid,
now I softly float to the parade;
down
down
down
where I'll play my part in the big show.
A happy end is in store, sometimes,
life inside a book of rhymes.
Where else is there to go?
Oh no, oh no,
you know what I'm talking about.

You may have thought but were not told,
the royal tomb is filled with fool's gold,
as all my dreams start to unfold;
down
down
down
unto passion's fertile ground.
Planted is our fantasia seed,
a natural form of greed
where my love is abound.

Ashes In My Skull

Oh yeah, oh yeah,
you know what I'm talking about.

Sometimes turmoil leads the way,
while science and religion teach you to pray,
for chaos and confusion to go away;
down
down
down
quietly the end has begun to form.
But the insanity tribe holds on desperately,
for I cannot be what I want to be,
a product of decorum.
Oh no, oh no,
you know what I'm talking about.

Candle of Chastity

The cabin fever unloads......
my dark side awakens
from its daylight hibernation,
(Euripides) somewhere back there;
enthralling nocturnal instincts,
I suppose that I really am insane.

Hovering girl......so sullen, so sedate,
I hate to see you masturbate.
The snug polished mould,
an imitation of delight;
portable foundations
for the lonely daffodil;
brings forth a chill......in Neptune.
The love you need is coming soon,
Lean back!

Remove the secret key
from around your waist;
frolicking debutante,
dressed in frills (and laced).
Now is the time
for virginity's resignation,
let yourself go unto denudation.

Passion turns to ecstasy,
midway through romance;
tonight you are mine,
I denounce your innocence.
Virgin in a frenzy, so savory......
squeezing out the isolation, delicately......
licking her lips; she slowly dips......
and the candle burns out.

Look at You, Look at Me

You know I usually hide
behind a glass curtain;
but this time I need you,
can't you see that I am hurtin'.
Share the pain, share the pain,
share the pain, share the pain.

It doesn't really matter,
why should I try?
You're just not that important
and, well......neither am I.
No one cares, no one cares,
no one cares, no one cares.

You could change the future,
and I could change the past;
but in a world full of losers,
we'd still be tied for last.
Look at you, look at me,
look at you, look at me.

Somehow, someway, somewhere,
I became so enchanted;
I fed you my life,
and you took it for granted.
Now it's gone, now it's gone,
now it's gone, now it's gone.

It will always linger on,
that crazy old love thing;
and now that I am buried,
the blackbirds, they shall sing.
Who is next, who is next,
who is next, who is next.

*Which is *Which

I'm *heart ached
I'm *misplaced

      a vindication of......despair,
      an action of......hope,
      a need for......death,
      the essence of......life,
      a salvation of......lust,
      the sanctity of......love,
      an asylum from......pain.

        Looking Up
        (stuck inside)
        Bogged Down

*a word of unknown origin
*a picture of a dead rose

        Subliminal insanity ~~~~~
        My mind is amiss ~~~~~~

And the first place I check is in my hand,
but the only way to find it, is in your kiss.
Unspoken chemistry, the exchange of vows,
a passage......to that which is left;
I cannot turn backward
but I am concerned about this

----------------------WALL----------------------
----

running straight through the sea;
a division of time and space,

*you | and | *me.

Monkey See, Monkey Do

It is all so precise and so true,
what monkeys see, monkeys do.

So I hide a raindrop
in the meadow.
Sparkling fantasy behind a tear;
everywhere
there are brainwashed people
hoping to nullify
each year.

Pinholes, lying,
frustrated women,
gladly pointing out
the forgotten sunshine.

Underneath the shadows of the ocean
next to your wide open tomb,
a palace of heartache and misfortune,
an endless empty path to eternity.

So the next time you see
happiness peeking
through a wormhole,
remember that it is just
a case of mistaken identity.

Go back to your song and dance,
boring places,
you are all the same to me.

Thomas Walker

This Girl is Just a Mirage

Everybody says I'm a loser,
       I'm lagging far/far behind;
everybody says I've got no feeling
       I'm just so/so unkind.
Everybody says the sun won't shine
       through the dark/darkened sky;
everybody says you can do what you want,
       all you have to do/do is try.

But I've been running through the desert,
       and it seems so/so insane;
I don't know how it happened
       but I found/found the rain.
So if you feel like giving up,
       won't you run/run with me;
but you had better bring your
       raincoat of mis/misery.

It's coming down hard now, it's coming down hard!
It's coming down hard now, it's coming down hard!

Now I may be unkind, but there's
       something I've got/got to say;
listen to me just this once
       and I'll be on/on my way.
You see you spend all your time
       and half/half you life;
running around looking for
       that per/perfect wife.

A girl off in the distance
       blinking all/all her lights;
ever so delicately searching
       for par/parasites.

Ashes In My Skull

Look at her, a glare across
      the blue/blue ocean;
look at her, in spite of all
      the com/commotion.

It's coming down hard now, it's coming down hard!
It's coming down hard now, it's coming down hard!

Don't forget that at the tips
      of the sand/sand filled dunes;
the scorpions are playing
      such love/lovely tunes.
But right around the corner glowing,
      is the girl/girl who sings;
immune to each and every one
      of the pois/poisoned stings.

The warm winds are blowing
      sand in to/to my face;
while shining eyes are keeping
      you in/in your place.
The sunrays creep through your window,
      outside it pours/pours down rain;
you lock yourself in and hide away
      all of to/today's pain.

It's coming down hard now, it's coming down hard!
It's coming down hard now, it's coming down hard

The Next Time I Blink

People say,
I must run away,
hide in a cave......
where I can write all day.
It is all in their eyes,
the cause of pray.

Utopia's flag is shrinking fast
as chaos wins......the system breaks down,
and gone is the motion that cons my ears to hear
a little blue lady saying,
I must sprinkle my heart with dust.
A fallen gleam, a chance to dream;
why answer a call from God,
look at me and give a nod.
Oh so tired, a place to sleep,
close my eyes, begin to weep.
Awake in time to settle down,
I could swim but choose to drown.
A mountain has begun to collapse,
a poet is at fault, perhaps.

The morning light is shining through,
and everyone wants to belong to everyone else.
Husbands, wives, lovers, romance.
the impotence of asceticism.
Open the door and let all in,
let us share the balances of life.
Petals fall on the orb sometimes,
I am sorry, and give up.
I give up on society, for now;
I am going to roam the worlds of north America
for a while,
and see where I am the next time I blink.

Just Like the Rest

She thinks she knows how to hate,
but of this I'll debate......
you see, sometimes I want her strangled,
she's often paranoid.
Platonic fantasies
invading......
fading......
in and out.
Does anybody really know me?
Does anybody think I care?
Anyone?
Anywhere?
Those 'Five Minutes' are gone
and don't mean a thing.
Do you believe in......a way?
Do you really think I care?
No one is above me but no one is below me;
and you still think you can show me......
the way.

I hear an angel screaming
somewhere beyond the dark.
She will not return this day in June,
nor will she return ever soon.
You......you never believed in me,
all the things that I said I could do.
Yeah, you never believed in me,
that my love could be so true.
So if you can show me that
you are not like all the rest,
then I will love you.
Then you can be like the rest,
and hurt me with your eyes......
and your emotion.

I Think that Someone is Following Me

Categorized by sleepless dreams,
we walk on needles......
(protruding from heartless eyes).

A savior always close behind,
slips

      i

        n

          to

            the

               p o   l   o
             o l o b o d   e l w
                   f   o   b   !

A mystified stranger shatters
his skull in disbelief;
and somewhere around
the great barrier reef,
an artist has given up......
(his quest for grief).

A Pair of Queens for Me

Golden paradise
across the sea,
I feel your sightline,
gazing at me.
Make the journey,
work your way through.
Bring your friend,
love can be two;
two queens
and a jester.
A couple of more souls
for the chastity molester.

Ride on Mighty Warrior

Ride on mighty warrior unto the sun,
a primitive religion, not new to science,
which venerates as though it were a deity.
I am your drug of unique distinction.
I am your mescaline, changing consciousness.
I am the hope that lies in the mirage ahead.

Ride on mighty warrior unto the sun,
you shall be noticed; there are many paths to God,
somewhere between universes,
often appearing incomplete or even non-existent.
But you share the limits of life's minute details,
the lovely gems and animated landscapes.

Ride on mighty warrior unto the sun,
vivid images of yesterday afternoon.
Whose land were you sleeping in,
where ghosts stood of burned flesh and blood,
thoughts becoming independent of life.
The faculty of visualization is unlimited, interesting
only when your temperature is high;
a desert heat felt at 3 1/2 m.p.h.

Ride on mighty warrior unto the sun,
bright nodes of energy swelling, expanding
in the red fire of magical growth;
plucking the petals of a flaming hue
from infinity's flower, moment by moment,
until left in a naked existence.
Follow the feathery incandescence,
ride on mighty warrior unto the sun.

The Labour of Man

The cavern deepens,
decaying......
with life's Unison Glory;
the brave abide with me,
rising......
with the forest moon.

I will tell you this,

> the dusky beach is
> the woman's noblest retreat,
> from the sky down to her feet;
> you never can tell her eyes
> from the thunder;
> the labour of man's whole life
> is to plunder.

Helpless and Hopeless

I often sit and wonder what I'm doing;
am I worth anything at all?
The pictures in my head are in motion,
a constant never-ending fall.

Who is who to say, what is beauty;
the impassioned transfer of a kiss.
Two young lovers strolling down the beach,
never knowing that one day they'll reminisce.

Dangerous ceremonies of heartache,
can you hear the pounding of the drums?
It is not how, why, or when......it just happens,
that wrenching pain behind your lungs.

They go by the names Helpless and Hopeless,
another two victims of the plague.
The rise and fall of expectations,
everything seems to be so vague.

The poet gives clues but not the answer,
the answer burns inside your head.
I hope you find all the puzzle pieces,
put them together, and then you're dead.

So the next time you meet......the one,
love them and leave them right away.
Because if you don't, then you will regret it,
every minute of every day.

A.K.A., the Praying Mantis

The devil's gatekeeper scored
and everyone roared;
seems like we've all been pulling
for the underdog lately.

The winds of indulgence are blowing hard,
knock you down when you're off guard;
but you always get back up
looking for the answer.

Look around, all you see is dirt
buried beneath all the hurt;
it is a simple, two-time ancient
modern contradiction.

Won't you take a ride on Neptune's seahorse,
he'll throw you spinning off course;
sometimes you have to go outside
the confines of acceptance.

You've seen the down side of down
when I said, let's leave this town;
but you've learned to turn your cheek
when it's not your problem.

So you would lay down real low
just watching your blood flow;
you were never one to be concerned
with my hungers.

Yeah you, you never wanted me,
you only wanted to get yourself free;
it's funny what people will do
for a piece of the action.

Thomas Walker

The rollercoaster is taking you up high,
more than halfway through the sky;
and you know that this time it's
going to be rough coming down.

But by now you should know, nothing matters
in a world filled with mad-hatters;
there is always someone waiting
just to push you over.

Pray that your taxi gets here on time
so you don't have to wait in line;
though you know that heaven
is right around the corner.

Look at the green grass growing,
feel the body juices flowing;
you've always known what
brings out the best in me.

There's a vacancy at body bag hotel,
down in the basements of hell;
someone has to pick up
all the pieces.

So if you really want to escape,
cut through all this red tape;
get out of here, get out
before you have to.

Something tells me you're not ready,
you're hand appears unsteady;
it must be that you're afraid to pull
the trigger on me.

They say that silence is golden
but look at the cards you were holdin';
you never had anything
to scream about.

Not everyone takes kindly to defeat
down on desperation street;
the snake always strikes
when backed into a corner.

So I'll just drift with the clouds,
stay away from the crowds;
for we are all saviors
when we are in isolation.

Just look, look for the ghost,
he's heading for the coast;
there's always been something sacred
about the ocean.

It is said that if you can make it there
then you can make it anywhere;
but I wonder if you can handle
the deepest darkest blue.

Do you know that down in Atlantis
they liken me to a praying mantis;
so you'd better not get
too close to me.

But I'd bet you'd like to find out
exactly what I am talking about;
so come and visit me,
my doors are always open.

A Trip to Venus

Naked Goddess surrounding me,
I don't care what you think, I've had too much to drink.
I am a passion poet; not like thee,
I can be anything I want to be.

Naked Goddess upon the stage,
I don't care what you think, I've had too much to drink.
Lasciviousness is pure; even for the sage,
who among us tries anything to rewrite the page.

Naked Goddess dance on my groin,
I don't care what you think, I've had too much to drink.
Don't be faint hearted; come and join,
you can do anything with the magic coin.

Naked Goddess your skin so sleek,
I don't care what you think, I've had too much to drink.
I am the one for you; not the meek,
I will do anything to make you peak.

Naked Goddess I'll take you home,
I don't care what you think, I've had too much to drink.
Lay your head back; look up to the dome,
you can do anything you please, when you are in Rome.

Naked Goddess your breasts so firm,
I don't care what you think, I've had too much to drink.
Be one with the serpent; glide and squirm,
do anything you want to release my sperm.

Naked Goddess you've let me in,
I don't care what you think, I've had too much to drink.
When juices are flowing; I will come again,
to give you anything, for a few hours of sin.

A Day With the Devil

A little town in Florida......
         where I held your hand;
         where I held your hand, babe;
         where I held your hand.
A little town in Florida......
         where I was your man.

But time passes by so mysteriously,
and the stars......they go away;
Oh, I'd give anything and twice as much,
to go back again......someday!

Thomas Walker

Alien Love Leaves Me Holding My Breath

She came from the stars with love in her eyes,
she came from the stars with love in her eyes.

It is no surprise, that people wonder
how it is that she flies
so high,
so high,
so high,
so high
so high,
with love at her fingertips,
with her love pressed against my lips,
oh, the eclipse,
oh, the eclipse.

Now I've slipped inside a dream
and inside of you I can see
that your heart is made of butterflies,
of roses, and of me.

What I think of you, you'll never know
because I'm afraid to tell you.
Yes, I'm afraid to tell you......
that you're my girl, you're my lover,
and I'm just afraid to blow my cover.
So I will hide instead
and make lies in my head.
How long must I tread
these waters; until I am dead?

I have my strengths.
I have my weaknesses,
and that is all you seem to notice......my weaknesses.
So I ask myself why, why should I care
if she is never there?

What I think of you, you'll never know
because I'm afraid to tell you.
Yes, I'm afraid to tell you......

so when I need a little
lo--------ve,
yes, when I need a little
lo--------ve,
you know where I will be!

Sometimes you have to swim down
way past reality;
so far that you can feel
the bottom of the sea;
down to the point where
you are not so sure
you will ever, ever, ever,
make it back......to her.

Thomas Walker

The Ecstasy of Salvation

The solitary mind shapes the spotlight world
eloquently in the night;
ceaseless tranquility,
the immortal sight.
Alone, we can be sufficient unto ourselves.
In the excavation of remembrance,
who can resist the azalea's company?

And so the elliptic patterning continues
for he who has nothing but epicurean fantasies.
After all, he who was born with nothing,
can do no worse than die with nothing.

Much greater disasters have struck mankind;
but I will tell you this,
fatality can be bliss.
Fatality will be mine,
for life vignettes......with time.

My Evening Lady

Is it good for you, or is it good for me?
Is it money well spent, or is this one for free?
I'm down when I'm uptown,
I'm up when I'm downtown.
I never know where I am......with my evening lady.

She says, you make me explode,
but you are not the only one.
You have to pay to play
with no guarantee for fun.
I said, you must be mistaking me
for one who wants you dressed in white.
The house is on fire,
let us keep it burning all night.
I'm down when I'm uptown,
I'm up when I'm downtown.
I never know where I am......with my evening lady.

The Birth

I've seen a lot of people,
I've seen a lot of misery,
and everywhere I go
the two are never apart.
Yeah, I have been
up and down the highways
looking for a heart.

At the time of my birth
the first image of the earth,
from the outside looking in.
Watching their heads spin
as they realized how small
they were, after all.

Because I am a ceremonial nightmare,
a 'gallery of despair'.
If I ever made love to a goddess,
the second coming of felicity.
Put your seat back,
take a look out of your sunroof,
It is raining isn't it......isn't it!

I don't love you
because you don't love me;
curious how the caged bird escapes
but does not always fly free.
He just sing, sings a song
about lonely misery.
He does not care about
Beowulf, Mona Lisa, or the Trinity.

Just because something is old
does not mean that it is made of gold,
you see!

Mama it's so cold,
won't you throw another blanket
onto me!

I think about the days that passed
searching for validity.
I've come a long way to escape
the outstretched arms of infinity
that took me to school, to learn the golden rule;
be all that you can be?
But when summer came around,
you were nowhere to be found.
You wouldn't fly away with me.
You would run around town
and kick me when I was down;
it was so easy.
You made some money quick,
as you took it from the sick
and the needy.
But I've got a gun,
and I'll fight for anyone
or anything, to be free.

Love can be bold,
tales of passion told,
deep within a fantasy.
Mama it's so cold,
won't you throw another blanket
onto me!

The White Rose

Sensual girl with the red dress, incognito,
Oh, how you move my libido
(when your long black hair touches me)
like a seismograph in a number 9.
Oh, how I'd like to taste your wine.
I've dreamed of you as cake,
devouring you in layers of ecstasy,
and making love to you
with fruitful delicacies
all around, their juices......oozing!
You have rescued me from
another lonely night.

Won't you come visit me again;
maybe we can be a star in the
erotic darkness;
and every now and then,
when we have nothing to offer
but death and desperation,
you can swallow the white rose petals.
You can make me feel so alive!
Stroke the stem, be careful of its thorns;
let the tip rest on your tongue,
and swallow the white rose petals;
I want to pollinate your mind.

The River

Temple of Eros;
paragon of ancient nudity,
your curves glisten in the sunshine.

If only I could sing
the song of 'Liaison';
tribal pageantry.

Let me be......be the judge
of your pleasantness;

your clean, shiny, flowing river
delivers my heart
insurmountable ecstasy.

Following the directions
on the treasure map,
in from behind
I've found a gap.

Down on your rapids
I lose control,
and in no time at all
I feed you my soul.

They called him……

The rain feels like glass
when you're lying on your bac
in the sand;
as the stars send out rumors,
that this whole damned thing
has been planned.
And sometimes you wander
off-course
thinking that you've got it all……
right in the palm of your hand.

The 'wild boy of Avaron' could not speak,
everyone called him a freak,
but when you'd get him cornered,
he would shriek.
You are the ones who are weak!
You are the ones who are weak!

Now life is life,
and all is said and all is gone,
and it is the memories of you,
that keep me going
on and on, on and on.

Hole in the Wall

The bridge from inside to outside is collapsing;
you know which bridge I am referring to,
the one from me to you.
Sometimes you have to live out a dream
to make a connection;
when the man and the woman are TWO,
then there is fear of death.
When ONE, then the dance of life.
And when your bridge is collapsing
from winds of fear
you know my shelter is always near;
fear not to be......
be naked amongst the light,
be ONE with the night.

Ask Jack, he will tell you,
it is easy to believe in the magic bean
when your head comes rolling off
the guillotine.
And I don't blame a single soul
for looking up to the fathom blue.
What else is there to do?
Oh, mystic rain,
every drop looks the same;
sundown gypsy woman,
I take you in my arms.

Riding through the desert
with her sitting at my side.
Signpost ahead......'roll on if you dare'.
I should have seen it coming,
the long and flowing hair;
Signpost ahead......'you'd best beware'
passion always rides down
the highway of despair.

oh, oh, oh, oh,
        ohthelightsarefeeling

STRONGER
       andtherazorbladelooks

L----O----N----G----E----R;

And the beast is hoping that
you're forever......
        on my mind,
        on my mind.

Do anything you'd like but
don't break my......
        heart again,
        heart again.

Yes, you know that her love brings
out the darkest (in my brain);
Oh yeah, you know her name,
I can just tell.
I don't know how to explain it,
I've got the talkin' dear John blues.
My baby left me for nothing,
now I've got nothing left to lose.
I feel like I'm walkin' thru the jungle
in the middle of the Vietnam War,
because when you've got nothing babe,
it cannot rain, it must pour.

I think I'll pull out my gun and fire
at the very next girl that I see
because every girl out there
reminds me of the way it used to be.
I know that you don't want much babe,
but then again, you took all that I had.
You left me out here like a rabid dog.
I think I'm going stark raving mad.

oh, if I told you
that I came here
just to say good-bye;
would you turn away,
would you turn away,
and begin to cry?

Desperate passion and a place to stay
It's a sacred way......
to the screaming islands,
I mean, the tearful soliloquy,
and the band of hate.
Look out mistress curiosity,
you might not like what you see;
the slipstream sanguine oil
is Satan's generosity;
but you cannot deny the opportunity
to......see me scream,
to......hear me dream.

Dear Mr. Mouse:

　　Thank you for letting me use
your hole in the wall. It was a little bit
tight but nice and cozy. Sorry about the
stain on your cat-skin rug. I made you a
cherry cheesecake, it's in the fridge. I'll
see you tomorrow.

　　　　　　　Your friend,
　　　　　　　Old Yeller

P.S. How old is your daughter? I'd like
to meet her some time, you know what
I mean?

Look Into the Sun

Two jobs, two ways;
each their own.
Is it all just a circumstance
now that their relationship
has become a mere acquaintance?

No time together,
no time to weather;
just another......Indian summer
in an ancient temple of love.

The intensity of love diminishes by the
Time Together Law.
As one begins to work in our society there is no time
left to unite with passion.
Love takes time
and time takes love......away from the heart.

A little confusing......
have we advanced?
Civilizations, machines, computers,
and do we save time?

~~~~~~~~~~~~~~~~~~~~~
Volcanoes of love spewing
                a hot liquid o'er
                the mountains of hope.
Civilized volcanoes spewing
                a gray ash o'er
                the hills of society.
~~~~~~~~~~~~~~~~~~~~~

But don't be so concerned
there is always time to hate.
It is so quick and easy.

It is a fast emotion,
a shotgun emotion,
an emotion for a civilized society.
Racing down the roads
day in, day out,
from sunset strip to the statue of liberty.

When you give up all
                conformist ways;
love is all there is
                to capture.

Once......

until your heart gets torn;
torn apart like a carcass on the plains
and left behind to be devoured by vultures.

You die.
You really die.

For this is death in its purest form.
The dream is recorded
and played back infinitely in the sun.
If you look, you will see

my heart in hell.

Thomas Walker

Mystic Sculptural Destiny of Dream

Oh, mystic sculptural destiny of dream.
Oh, mystic sculptural destiny of dream.

I stand here fully erect, my head through the seam;
with my magic upon her, eyes sparkle and gleam;
of the mystic sculptural destiny of dream.

And I come to the shadow of her rainbow's beam;
where eternity does flow in a soft white stream;
by the mystic sculptural destiny of dream.

The mind fills with euphoria, the heart does scream;
as she finds herself covered in moonlight's cream;
from the mystic sculptural destiny of dream.

I Can't Make Up My Mind

And if you keep on saying
whooo------oooa, maybe, I guess, I don't know;
then you'll wind up lonely in the end.
And if you keep on saying
whooo------oooa, do I really love her;
then you'll wind up lonely in the end.
That is for sure, that is for sure.
And sometimes I just want to kill, me sometimes me.
And sometimes I want to kill, you sometimes you.
Passion is god, god is frustration.
Love lies, love lies,
love lies, love lies,
silently in pain.

When you've seen an ocean tumble and crawl,
you wonder what is happening down the hall.
Why is there screaming?
At the point of insertion, a funny feeling in my bones,
hidden in the passion of the thrashing and the moans.
So safe and so secure; every man wants to wander through
islands of women with nothing to do.
Sex is in the air;
indulging in forbidden treasures,
the lovely insidious pleasures.
We'll make love here and there,
we'll make love everywhere;
nothing less than sacred.

And sometimes I just want to kill, me sometimes me.
And sometimes I want to kill, you sometimes you.
Passion is god, god is frustration.
Love lies, love lies,
love lies, love lies,
silently in pain.

Loveinarose

Love is not a diamond ring,
it does not last forever.

Love is not a one night fling,
only to sever.

Love is not a long white dress,
it is not pure.

Love is not meant to impress,
it is to endure.

And
I love you for real,
that is for sure.

Only you can make me feel,
only you can steal
my heart
even when we are apart;
I love you for real.

The Darkest Day of the Year

One day the cries will amorphosize
from the 'Garden of Laughters';
a tenacious two-some, down from the rafters.
Let us decide the palace of revelry;
between her lips, the devil's adversary.

Autumn's beauty anchors with divinely sedation
in the oasis of blue rocks, blue ice, and burning;
love letters yearning
to cultivate a new harvest.

Take me into your room, quilted goddess
and let me explore your form;
for black is the good-bye that I forlorn.
So hold me, the travelling prisoner,
unto that wintery day in December;
remember, my dear,
I am the Neptune King,
born on the darkest day of the year.

What does it matter?

The rain keeps pouring down
yet seems so far away;
pain going beyond suffering
into the valley of agony.
Dredging up the bottom,
bottom of the sea;
I long to have you near,
sit down beside me.
The lightning storm defines
all that I am.
Down another river of hope,
blocked by a damn.

Now you may never be the president,
but you can surely make a statement.
You may never be a Michelangelo,
but you can always be a child's hero.

What does it matter?
It is all the same,
what does it matter?

Now you may never be a rock-n-roll star,
but you can sing along in your car.
You may never unite the golden mate,
but you can always self satiate.

What does it matter?
It is all the same,
what does it matter?

The Sad Clown

Please let down your hair,
I like it long and flowing free.
Every time I go outside
I somehow think I'm going to die;
but these thoughts are not in fear,
for I cannot fear my one and only.

She is so close to me now.

I'd like to take a walk downtown
where everybody laughs at the clown,
but me......I'll just sit and stare.
I see a jet go by in my head,
and wonder if my girl is dead.
If so, I wish that I were there;
have a drink and laugh a while
and see if you can get in style.
Tell me......
have you a few minutes to spare?
Have another drink and relax a while,
see if you can notice a smile.
Look for the girl with long black hair.

It does not matter
whether you win or lose
because in the end,
only the kings
will be remembered.
Staggering tendencies of light,
brightness everywhere,
brightness everywhere,
and you know, it is not fair,
but only if you make it there,
So save all your money for the heir,
then he or she might make it there.

115

And the next time you are down
strolling around some lonely town,
looking up from the ground;
you will see them laugh at the clown.
Even the one with the frown.
Everybody get way down
because I think I am going to kill
a dream or two,
like you......out of spite.
It doesn't matter, wrong or right.
What goes through your head......
at night?
Does the thought of death......
bring fright?

I did not want to come here anyway,
let us leave this party early.
I know a place where we can be alone,
gaze at the future,
see the cracks in the bone.

Erotic destiny you are mine
I have left the party on time.
I do not care about people,
I could live in isolation.
I am a midnight rambler,
believe in desolation.
I need a few minutes
to think about life.
I need a few minutes
to sharpen its knife.
It is going to take all day
to kill......if I do it my way.

I said, I have no ambition
and I don't want your money,
God damn,
God damn,
God damn.

Ashes In My Skull

She said, I hate you
and I don't want you around,
just go away,
just go away,
just go away.

So weave me a noose,
try not to make it too loose
and the next time you see me
sitting at Devil's Lake,
take a picture of me
for God's sake.

I say there is more to life
than the physical world around you;
feel the invisible snake
slithering,
slipping through
doorways that are new.

Let the hissing continue......

and take you away
with the cavern dwellers;
for there is no future in the past,
the smallest of shadows is cast.

Let the hissing continue......

Act VII - I Remember Days

The next ------ time,
the next ------ time,

I fly into your dreams;
I want to see,
I want to see.

Life,
it is just a put on babe,
an act of verity, an act of verity.

I remember days, I remember days,
when I felt like a born loser.
I remember days, I remember days,
when I thought I was a spy.

I remember days, I remember days,
when I hated you so very much.
I remember days, I remember days,
when I thought that I'd never die.

I remember days, I remember days,
when I wanted to kill myself in shame.
I remember days, I remember days,
when I thought I'd cracked life's mystery.

I remember days, I remember days,
when I envisioned colors and swirl.
I remember days, I remember days,
when I founded ancient history.

I remember days, I remember days,
when I was as cold as Alaska.
I remember days, I remember days,
when I was overflowing with care.

I remember days, I remember days,
when I drifted like a feather.
I remember days, I remember days,
when I couldn't go anywhere.

I remember days, I remember days,
when I washed away like a sand castle.
I remember days, I remember days,
when I was a strong as a mountain.

I remember days, I remember days,
when I could not find any love.
I remember days, I remember days,
when I exploded like a fountain.

So,
the next ------ time,
the next ------ time,
I fly into your dreams;
I want to see,
I want to see.
Life,
it is just a put on babe,
an act of verity,
an act of verity.

(is it just another barroom scene?)

Ad infinitum;
you build the fires and I'll light'em.
When you're feeling so low,
take your fist and hit the ground below.
I want you to know

you can come see me.

If you don't know what to do;
your dreams are all in blue,
blue and white, blue and white.
Your dreams are all of sky,
desolate sky.

It keeps you so uptight,
it disguises all the light,
sometimes it makes you think that night is......
               all around you,
               all around you.
You are just another mole,
and blindness is your role,
so you'd better dig another hole......
               for your body,
               for your body.
You know I've had it up to here,
with the small talk and the beer,
where everybody lives in fear......
               of the future,
               of the future.
I see them all smoking,
I see them all joking,
and everyone of them is choking......
               on their dream,
               on their dream.

Oh What a (　　) Feeling

To come back down
before you've touched the ceiling;
I thank you for everything,
(((dead in the barn, - - - ((the chains,
they are rusted and creaking.

I've got some ideas......
put some more splatters of blood
on the shady porch,
and put on your bonnet,
(like a lady in days of old).

Go cut yourself a block of ice,
a huge block of ice.
Set it outside and watch it
melt for a few years;
it is so very hot this summer.

She said, you know......
my teapot whistles 'Bolero'
I said, well then......
how about some tea?)) - - -

you are a very beautiful woman,
and it breaks my heart to tell you
that I have nothing to offer)))
except this bag of sand.

Thomas Walker

I am the Butterfly

Her walls filled with schizophrenic art;
she shares......shares the darkness
with those who are friends.
Fly by her window in the darkness......
of a warm night.

She catches a butterfly in mid-flight,
and out of mind, yet still in sight,
is the safety of tomorrow,
with her reflections.....flowery and soft.

The Stowaway

The sun always kills /
        by surprise.
Look into my eyes /
        a bleeding fool, who'll
do anything for you......(duel?)
I am sure you are glad that I am not around
        to annoy you,
        to deploy you,
        to destroy memories
        (the parasite) of heartache.
Girl from the north,
why must you terrorize
love......until it dies?
The first few seconds of creation
(an unexpected place in the universe)
are transfixed by the night sky,
        and a kiss on the lips.
A glimpse of hope feeds the eye;
        the presence of happiness slips,
        and leaves me witnessing
        the unimportance of mankind's history.
I am just a stowaway on the island of fear.
Life is full of explosions and great events,
        far and near;
but only in death can you see
        through a new light.
Only in death can you see......
        beyond sight.
So kick me in the face, I want to leave;
there is nothing worse than waking up.
I prefer death, like rain;
        no dreams, no hope,
        just death, just sleep.

Another Day at Work

I'm gonna tell ya about a working man,
I'm gonna tell ya the best I can.

> Strange majestic purple weed;
> how many people do you feed?
> He worked and sang till all was gone;
> he worked and sang till nobody cared.

Woke up yesterday,
woke up just to pray
that I wouldn't have to stay......here much longer,
that I wouldn't have to be here today.
I don't think I can take it anymore.
I've been banging my head against the door......
of opportunity.
You know what's killing me?

Just turned twenty-five and I'm in a rut.
Twenty-five years of school, so now what?
Which wrist is the first to cut......
the last to bleed.

When I was a child,
a soldier of the night,
people would tell me
that I didn't know wrong from right.
Now that I'm older, I make all the rules.
Now who is laughing?
Now you are the fools.

Now all day I just lay in bed.
I would get up but my feet feel like lead.
I am just looking for a 'pains taker',
a woman who knows my name;
a woman who desires everything the same.

Ashes In My Skull

I don't know what happened to me,
but I just don't care about 'the things' anymore.

The walls, the skin, the food, the color, the beer,
the toys, the picture, the bed, the water, the fear;
I have to get out of here.
I don't want to play
your reindeer games anyway.
Did you ever take a week......or even a day,
where you did not utter a single word;
and not another voice was heard?

I think I'll go hitchhike around the world
and come back with my life unfurled.

Bizarre worlds of life, evolving from death

An affirmation of death
expectation......
    expectation of hope;
lustful dreams,
    now is the time to help.

READY,
SET......
LEARN!!!

Learning is fun.
Learn to earn.
Learn to die......
    or just die.
A strange doctor has come to your aid;
the funny thing though,
he is no doctor of medicine.
He is a doctor of love (poet).

Neptune calling regularly to kill places
that you've been, but could never be;
    shadows,

    ~

    ~

    ~

    alone,
nothing beats protection.

Everybody wants to be a gun-shooting hero;
rescuing whores from the dark side of town.
And wherever you are with true eyes shining,
you are never far from a whore and a gun.
So go and give back all of your borrowed time.
Now is the time to get something done.

Ashes In My Skull

Sometimes I get caught behind a wheel,
you know how it makes me feel,
you know how it makes me feel.

Sometimes I get high and think about feeling
and say, "what is wrong?"
I lay in bed and stare at the ceiling
and say "what is wrong?"
Take a walk outside and look at the stars
and say, "what is wrong?"
I gaze into the mirror, straight through my eyes
and say, "what is wrong?"

Is there any hope down this darkened alleyway?
Is there any hope in these words today?

But you know that......
hope is just another configuration of pain,
                    flowing down the drain of life;
and you know that......
hope is just another celebration of disdain,
                    rolling across the terrain of death.

Who really gives a damn anyway,
I sure as hell don't.
I don't care what any damn thing,
resembling any kind of life or death,
in any kind of universe,
does......or doesn't do!!!

Love is an Art (for some I say)

We bathed together
in an ancient pool
in our younger days of school.

The serpent arose from the sea,
it came to join you and me
in the 'great juncture'
which set us free.

Now if the stairway you are on
ascends at ninety degrees,
you can't ask for much
you must be easy to please.

So when you are
'wanted: for love'
get down on your knees
and passionately tell
the story of......
romance in an eggshell.

Talking Newspaper Blues

Step out into the abbreviated night
outside your newspaper cabin.
Where is everybody?
All wrapped up in the obituaries
or maybe the comics; shoot a smile.
Spin the globe slowly until you find where you are,
some kind of unending ordeal is in your pockets;
stick your hands inside and find it.
Put some steak in your mouth;
it is a big world isn't it.
Make a fist, shake it,
and enjoy as you watch lady Godiva
stroll up and down and up and down
the block......everybody's nervous, sweating,
thinking she might want a lover;
some kind of a hard man
with heavy comprehension
of what a lady needs......idealized admiration
leading to an encounter of vicious desperation.
After all......it is what a man has to be.
Open up your window, over by the want ads;
everything that you desire,
everything is for sale, Mrs. Summer.
Some kind of blue-eyed weak failure
or a bunny rabbit and a diamond ring,
or how about some human jelly
but don't show anyone.
Tear a leaf from an ugly plant
and do not apologize
because you don't like me anyway,
and you know we always have to pay......
for a companion.
A donkey ride into the canyon
where we play hide and seek,
separating the strong from the weak.

Go turn on the television,
over by the wedding pictures;
a movie house of love with more magic
than Merlin in a cloud of dust.
A white knight in shining armor
polishes his own sword so it won't rust,
but he doesn't call it lust; just a simple lack of trust.
Casanova drinking from the fountain
runs around the wheel like a lab rat,
afraid he will get fat, and never see them anymore.
Because they are oh so tanned,
and they don't have to use their hand,
or any kind of tools to polish all their jewels.
And like the little pussycat,
she too, is worried that she's fat.
She distrusts everything and everyone,
and even most of herself.
She keeps her dreams upon the shelf......
right by the sports section.
Can you tell me, who is number one,
who finished first, and who will finish last?
It is the society of battle; is it really just a game?
The throbbing and the perfume,
the flashing of her necklace,
and the feel of her dress;
look at the eagerness in his face
hoping to see some lace,
hoping that he'll win......the race.
She said, I hope you are having a good time
because it is a good time to go, go home.
You always increase my respiration;
faster and faster, heart palpitation,
leaving me in another sticky situation
lying on my back in milky isolation.
Go downstairs and get me some juice,
over by the stock exchange;
the flood is receding, extravagance is strange.
Buy them when they are low, low,
and sell them when they are high, high;

if you are in trouble
sometimes it is a good thing to laugh.
All dried up inside, unemotional people
sell for fun, sell for the steeple;
every day in modern America
another caesarean born millionaire;
seven pounds, eight ounces,
blue eyes, and dark brown hair.
Practice, practice, practice, until you get it right;
the sun is always shining, but there isn't always light.
Go outside and get some logs for the fire;
the more that you use,
the flame will grow higher.
Good-bye newspaper,
good-bye gossip words;
watch them disappear,
watch them by the herds
walking around with blinders.
You've suddenly walked off the cobbled street.
Can you hear the ice of life cracking beneath your feet?
It all comes too soon, the taste is bittersweet;
some of us believe that you get back all you give,
but it doesn't work out that way when you choose to live
with a lady that you'd die for, a lady that you love;
wherever wings are clipped, you find a lonesome dove.
Look at the front page headlines,
momma kills her little girl, momma kills her little boy,
daddy kills momma, then kills himself too;
and turn to the last page, Macy's is having a sale.
You can get dressed for half price,
they will keep you looking nice;
and somewhere in the middle, in fine print,
maybe you can read it,
but you'll have to squint......your weary eyes.
Nobody really cares: another poet dies.

Smiling Young Princess

I'd give up all the good memories
to rid of all the bad.
For those are the memories,
the memories that make me mad.

But I shall not anticipate
the young princess smiling
(I soon will miss).
The morning comes in time, she said,
leaving her hand to kiss.
Present situations bear the weight;
a flourishing condition
perhaps obtained too soon.

What words are these,
during a course of trouble?
Hoping times watching the rain,
watching the rain, watching the rain.
Peeking through a window,
a white canary is singing;
free from falling the water.

These are colloquial times,
man says to Woman.
Your brain will get you nowhere,
woman says to Man.
And who put me in charge of the frenzy;
he who said, they would invent Him?
Another man who read another's life,
not a poet.
And for all of this nonsense
it is not the poet, but the Muse,
who must analyze the blues.

Jealousy's Mistress

You keep polishing empty pulsating dreams
      hoping she will never fade.
But the ribbons and bows
      and clothes
      she wears, they hide the things inside.
The things that make the angels
      weep and moan,
      thrown together, desecrate they can
the foundations of a man;
      but distraught, I move on
until gone, the hope
      of holding on to the next rope.

You will come in alone, you will go out alone,
and all you can do in between is learn.
If I have to die, I want you there by my side.
It is like any other religion;
something you turn to that makes
you feel safe and secure.
That is why you love her.

You feel as though you have to confer;
I am not saying, this is bad,
I am not saying, this is good,
I am just saying, this is true.
That is why I love you.

It is like any other religion;
something you turn to that makes
you feel safe and secure.
Many things fall into place
to make you feel sure;
put the puzzle together,
the last piece is the cure.

So if you want a lot and you get a lot,
then you are happy.

If you don't want much and you don't get much,
then you are happy as well.

I don't know why I am dying,
I am not like all the rest;
I don't see any use in trying
to find that treasure chest.
Sometimes it makes you so sad
and you wish that you were blessed
with the happiness of knowing
that you are nothing but a guest.

I am just another lonely poet
who lives in a sketchbook,
a world of ideas,
unfinished and pure.

Always waiting around
beneath the sun's light
with not a possibility in sight.
Woman dressed so tight
with your hair dyed raven black;
how I'd like to take you......
take you in the back,
and love you
to orgasmic symphonies
again and again,
Ms. Erotica,
again and again.

When I am finished with you,
finished,
the end;
I will consider you a friend.
through the doorways I shall send
you calling my name.

Defend your vows when no one knows;
the girl that gets, is the girl that goes......
looking for life as she swallows
molecular infinity, and filling the void,
a virginal body, fate hath destroyed.

Struck down by the splendors of noonday,
the prize and pleasures of perfection
peering through the dungeon gates;
drunken in my dreams,
my grave awaits......
to entertain me
in the methods of an old passion
forming through a spire of hope.
Duty cries aloud,
"knowledge is jealousy's mistress,
in a land of lost repent."

With no magic left in her smile
she closes in on an ancient isle.
Spurned in vain, her fondness released;
rough and used, her beauty deceased.

Here Lies......Melinda

All asleep,
all in too deep,
AWAKE!
Sided by the beast,
join us in our feast.

Who so condemns me, the night-wind composer,
for uttering words of passionate somber?
Crawl back inside my brain;
look into my eyes, can you feel the pain?
Love is a wedge,
way back in your soul of dream.
I'll take my ax in so deep,
it will make you scream.

People say that she's a savior,
but not when she's on her best behavior.
She has saved so many one-way lives
with just a simple glare of her eyes.
Melinda loves the life that she lends
to her dearest, closest friends.

Needles and pins protrude a life-size doll
strolling down the mirrored hall;
the voodoo images no one wants to pass
until they look into the glass.
Reflections so clear, what is there to do
when they all look exactly like you.

Satiated moments so few and far between;
I get the feeling nobody knows what I mean.
But never, never are you solely
in a world going down slowly;
and sometimes you feel like a loser,
a psychotic pattern abuser.

---Slow down for me.---
---Slow down for me.---

Lovely lady and her moistened lips
conjure up sunken fantasy ships.
---Slow down for me.---
---Slow down for me.---

My six-shot camera of posterity
senses epitaph writings for humanity.
---Slow down for me.---
---Slow down for me.---

Strangely though, a hidden flow of brain semen
unloads reality onto the face of the demon.
---Slow down for me.---
---Slow down for me.---

The sanctuary of dichotomy begins to sting,
and out of the deck comes the suicide king.
---Slow down for me.---
---Slow down for me.---

There always has to be an end to the story,
melting icicles bring forsaken glory.

Thomas Walker

Infant Sorrow

So if you really love her,
then why don't you kill her?
Kill her......while you can.
She may seem so happy,
she may seem so kind,
but in the end......she's just a woman.

I think I'll go relinquish myself
to slumberous times;
my ship of dreams is sailing
through an ocean full of mines.
I think I'll go tell everybody
what they already know;
that nothing and nothing
leaves you with nowhere to go.

No more promises by the hour.
No more grapes to turn sour.
Can you see my signals of distress?
Come and get me out of this mess.

They follow along
one by one by one;
downtown by the bay,
where they make their run
to the sultry, sullen,
sanguine shine
in the sun.
And you say, who am I
to ridicule; to put you on trial.
But I did not ask you to come here,
I did not ask you to smile.
So just sit there
and shake your heads
for a while.

Ashes In My Skull

She said, let's go out drinking.
I said, shhhhhh, I'm thinking.
Up on the roadside, a desert café;
nothing is there, but stop anyway.

We need to take a trip, and take it soon.
We need to take a trip down to Neptune.
The treacherous journey coming to a halt;
you can't blame anyone, it's nobody's fault.

Tired of hanging around, life's not amusing;
not having any fun, it's all so confusing.
Tired of hanging around for everyone I've met;
and all I've ever wanted but could not get.

When you're born, two lives you are given;
one is for learning, one is for living.
You're here today, and you're gone tomorrow.
Oh where are you going, infant sorrow?

The Last Serenade

Take me......take me away.
Oh, won't you take me away.
Take me tomorrow or take me today;
whatever you do, just take me to stay.

Take me......to your palace of love;
you know where I'm thinking of.
Beautiful white winter dove,
please take me away!

Take me......gently by the hand;
down into the promise land.
Bury my head in the sand,
please take me away!

Take me......take me away.
Oh, won't you take me away.
Take me tomorrow or take me today;
whatever you do, just take me to stay.

Take me......goddess of serenity;
no one's to know but you and me.
Where life is flowing free,
please take me away!

Take me......my one and only girl;
my mind begins to swirl.
Fountains of shapeless pearl,
you take me away!

Take me......take me away.
Oh, won't you take me away.
Take me tomorrow or take me today;
whatever you do, just take me to stay.

About the Author

The author is alive.
The author has been woken.

Thomas Walker Publications

Eagle River, Alaska